AF228485

Ways of Seeing

For Hugh

*Pentru rugăciunile Sfinţilor Părinţilor noştri,
Doamne Iisuse Hristoase Fiul lui Dumnezeu,
miluieşte-ne pe noi. Amin.*

Ways of Seeing

*Orthodox Spirituality for
Our Modern World*

Nevsky Everett

CANTERBURY
PRESS

© Nevsky Everett 2026

First published in 2026 by the Canterbury Press Norwich

Editorial office
3rd Floor, Invicta House
110 Golden Lane,
London EC1Y 0TG, UK
www.canterburypress.co.uk

Canterbury Press is an imprint of Hymns Ancient & Modern Ltd
(a registered charity)

Hymns Ancient & Modern® is a registered trademark of
Hymns Ancient & Modern Ltd
13A Hellesdon Park Road, Norwich,
Norfolk NR6 5DR, UK

All rights reserved. No part of this publication may be reproduced,
stored in a retrieval system, or transmitted,
in any form or by any means, electronic, mechanical,
photocopying or otherwise, without the prior permission of
the publisher, Canterbury Press.

Nevsky Everett has asserted his right under the Copyright, Designs and Patents
Act 1988 to be identified as the Author of this Work

Scripture quotations are from New Revised Standard Version Bible: Anglicized
Edition, copyright © 1989, 1995 National Council of the Churches of Christ in
the United States of America. Used by permission. All rights reserved worldwide.

British Library Cataloguing in Publication data

A catalogue record for this book is available
from the British Library

ISBN: 978-1-78622-706-5

EU GPSR Authorised Representative
LOGOS EUROPE, 9 rue Nicolas Poussin, 17000, LA ROCHELLE, France
E-mail: Contact@logoseurope.eu

No part of this book may be used or reproduced in any manner for the purpose
of training artificial intelligence technologies or systems.

Typeset by Regent Typesetting

Contents

Acknowledgements

This book began life as a series of retreat addresses for the Chaplaincy of Christ Church, Vienna. I'm grateful to Fr Patrick Curran for the invitation, and to him and his congregation for their warmth and kindness. Likewise, Fr Richard Stanton invited me to lead a short retreat using these talks at St John the Baptist, Timberhill with St Julian's in Norwich. My own congregation in Bucharest was gracious enough to hear some of this material as part of a Lenten series on Orthodox spirituality. The feedback I received was generous and helpful.

As I have made myself at home in Romania and have come to understand the lived experience of Orthodoxy, I am indebted to many people for their openness and generosity. His Beatitude Patriarch Daniel and those hierarchs of the Holy Synod of the Romanian Orthodox Church whom I have met have all been kind to me and I am thankful to them. I would particularly like to thank Fr Michael Tiţa, Fr Augustin Coman, Fr Gabriel Cazacu and Fr Mihai Spătărelu for all their help in navigating the Orthodox and ecumenical landscape. Dr Aleandru-Marius Crişan has been a good friend and fellow ecumenist.

Some of my most profound experiences of the Byzantine tradition in Bucharest have been in the Greek Catholic Cathedral not far from our church. Bishop Mihai Frăţilă and his clergy have been exceptionally kind neighbours.

Last, I would like to thank Clare and our children, Agnes, Alban and Ephrem. Even if they think that I have too many icons and too many Orthodox liturgical books, their willingness and support in our Romanian adventure have been an inspiration. Toată dragostea mea.

Preface

Having the name 'Nevsky', after the thirteenth-century Russian prince St Alexander Nevsky, I have always been interested in Russian culture specifically, and Orthodoxy more widely. I have had many failed attempts at learning Russian, but my experiences and encounters with the Orthodox Church (largely outside the Russian context) have stuck with me. One of my first adult encounters with Orthodoxy was when Metropolitan Kallistos Ware preached in the chapel of my undergraduate college. He was gracious, funny and wise, and made a deep impression. I remember going straight from dinner that evening to the college library to see what they had on Orthodoxy.

Since then, I have always been around Orthodox churches. There was a Russian Orthodox congregation that met in the chapel of my theological college, and a Serbian Orthodox congregation that worshipped once a month in the church where I was a curate. I learnt Syriac as an ordinand and came into sustained contact with the Syrian Orthodox Church (which belongs to the Oriental Orthodox family of churches, along with the Armenian, Ethiopian and Coptic churches). I was pleased to serve for a while as the Anglican Co-Secretary of the Anglican-Oriental Orthodox Regional Forum. My doctorate was on St Isaac of Nineveh, widely venerated in the Eastern Orthodox Church, but himself a bishop of the Assyrian Church of the East. As a chaplain in Oxford, I attended the Greek, Russian and Romanian parishes, and I was a trustee of the House of St Gregory and St Macrina, an important and venerable centre of ecumenical encounter.

It was, however, only after leaving Oxford for Bucharest that I have come to live in the Orthodox world and to see the lived experience of Orthodoxy as it is in Romania. As the Archbishop of Canterbury's Apokrisarios (a grand Byzantine title meaning 'representative'!) to the Romanian Orthodox Patriarchate, I have been privileged to take part in many formal meetings and events alongside the bishops and clergy of the Romanian Orthodox Church. But that alone would only tell half a story. I have learnt just as much about the lived experience of Orthodoxy from the people I meet around churches and monasteries, from visitors to our own church in Bucharest, even from people I meet in the park or at the market. The warmth, generosity and openness of ordinary Romanians, as well as their piety, has made a deep impression on me.

This book is an attempt to communicate some of the ways that my understanding and vision of the Christian life has been changed by my sustained encounter with Orthodoxy. It is, therefore, a personal account rather than a comprehensive introduction to the belief and practice of the Orthodox Church. Each chapter draws on an aspect of Orthodox spirituality that has taught me to see things in a new way. It is also worth noting that I have written this book as an outsider. I am an Anglican who has come to love Orthodoxy, and that too will no doubt have coloured my reflections. It is a book that seeks to share the riches of the Orthodox tradition as I have experienced them with a non-Orthodox audience. I hope that in these pages, the reader will find something of value that will spur them on to their own encounters with the beauty, faithfulness and richness of the Orthodox Church.

Foreword

It was with great pleasure that I received the invitation to write a foreword to this wonderful book, which offers an overview of some of the riches of Orthodox spirituality and their relevance to the contemporary world. I consider the publication of this book by Fr Nevsky Everett a major event, especially due to its profound engagement with crucial aspects of the mystical and ascetic practice of Orthodox Christianity.

In so doing, Fr Nevsky Everett's *Ways of Seeing* continues with success a beautiful tradition inaugurated by one of his famous predecessors at the Anglican church in Bucharest, namely Father Hugh Wybrew, who served the Anglican community in the capital city of Romania decades ago and authored several excellent monographs on Orthodox Christianity, particularly on its Liturgy. I have no doubt that Fr Nevsky Everett's book is going to enjoy the same popularity and prestige among Western and Eastern Christian theologians, scholars and believers.

The relevance of this book is at least twofold. First, it captures the beauty of Orthodox spirituality with the freshness that only a non-Orthodox could attempt. However, the benefit goes both ways. It is not only Orthodox Christianity that benefits from the publication of such a book, as it sees itself through the eye of the Christian other; but the author himself is enriched by the encounter with Orthodox spirituality, as he acknowledges in the introduction to the book. This publication is therefore one of the many fruits of a transformative encounter. This is why the book speaks both to the mind and the heart. Given Fr Nevsky Everett's profound reflections and genuine testimonies, I am convinced that many readers will appreciate the depth of the message conveyed by this book and the beauty of a Christian tradition that has a lot to offer to the modern world.

Second, the book is an exercise in ecumenical thinking and reflection, for it generously guides those who are not familiar with Orthodox Christianity through the complexities of its spirituality. The book is more than an ecumenical introduction into Orthodox spirituality for a contemporary audience. It is a solid theological analysis undertaken in order to 'discover spiritual treasures that help us to see things in new ways, making visible the transforming power of Christ's Resurrection, and drawing us into the life of the Kingdom of God in the here and now'. I personally wish Eastern theologians would engage with Anglican spirituality with the same passion and interest that Fr Nevsky Everett engaged with Orthodoxy.

This book by Fr Nevsky Everett is an ecumenical gift to be cherished and praised. I cannot but congratulate the author and hope that other fruits of his encounter with Orthodoxy will be made available to us in the future.

Archimandrite Dr Augustin (Viorel) Coman

Introduction

For many Christians from Catholic and Protestant backgrounds, Orthodoxy has an exoticism and mystery about it that can be either attractive or off-putting, according to temperament. Our knowledge and experience will vary significantly, depending on whether we have an Orthodox parish near where we live, or perhaps whether we have taken an interest in Orthodoxy online. Our first experiences of Orthodoxy will likely highlight those things that are unfamiliar or that feel to us in some way 'Eastern'. It might be the sight of frescoed churches full of icons, the icon screen that shields the sanctuary from our view, the sound of Byzantine chant or a liturgical language that somehow even sounds ancient. But if we are able to look beyond what seems new and strange to us, to get to know it, then the Orthodox tradition offers us spiritual treasures that can open our eyes to the presence of God in the world, drawing us into a more profound understanding of the Church and even of ourselves.

The term 'Eastern Orthodox' refers to a communion of self-governing ('autocephalous') or autonomous churches, each with its own language, history and customs. The faith of these churches is rooted in the Scriptures, in the writings of the Church Fathers and in the doctrinal statements of the seven ecumenical councils (the first was in AD 325 and the last in AD 787). The importance of this unity in belief and practice is underlined by the fact that the word 'Orthodox' means 'true' or 'correct' (*orthos*) 'belief' or 'worship' (*doxa*).

Today, there are some 260 million Orthodox Christians and Orthodox parishes can be found all over the world, from Alaska to Japan. Roughly 75% of the world's Orthodox Christians, however, live in Central and Eastern Europe.[1]

From the time of the Emperor Justinian (d. 565), the Church was governed by the five Patriarchs of Rome, Constantinople, Alexandria, Antioch and Jerusalem. Until the Great Schism of 1054, the Bishop of Rome was preeminent among them, and after the separation of Rome, the Patriarch of Constantinople (the Ecumenical Patriarch) was seen as the first among equals. There is no central authority within Orthodoxy, as there is in the Roman Catholic Church. The Ecumenical Patriarch is simply the first in honour among the other heads of self-governing Orthodox churches. In this way, the Anglican Communion shares a similar ecclesiological outlook, with the Archbishop of Canterbury as the spiritual leader of a number of self-governing national and regional churches.

Over time, the historical heartlands of Orthodoxy shifted away from modern Turkey and the Middle East, though the ancient Christian communities of these lands still bear witness to the faith, after centuries of persecution and even genocide.[2] Christianity took root among the Slavic peoples of Central and Eastern Europe in the ninth century, through the missionary activity of the brothers Cyril and Methodius from Thessalonica. The Southern Slavic Kingdoms of Bulgaria and Serbia converted to Christianity, and, around the year 988, Prince Vladimir the Great was baptized, and Kievan Rus' with him. Following the Fall of Constantinople in 1453 to the Ottomans, the Orthodox Church in Moscow became increasingly aware that it was the only place in the Orthodox world that was politically independent. The Russian Church became self-governing in 1589, declaring the Russian Tsardom the 'third Rome'.

With the changing geopolitical realities of the nineteenth and twentieth centuries in Eastern Europe, a number of national churches gained (or regained) their independence, namely the Orthodox Churches of Greece, Serbia, Romania, Bulgaria, Poland, Georgia and Albania. In the political upheaval of that time, the question of autocephaly was closely connected with the right to self-determination at the national level. This issue continues to be a political one, as is painfully apparent in Ukraine.

In some ways, the picture is even more complicated outside Orthodoxy's historic homelands. In many cities in Western Europe and the United States over the course of the tumultuous twentieth century, Orthodox parishes were set up for diaspora communities. This has continued with the accession of Orthodox-majority countries to the European Union and the Schengen Area. These parishes maintain the liturgical language, culture and traditions of the national churches from which they came, but have increasingly had to adapt to shifting demographics, an increase in the use of the English language and converts from outside their ethnic communities.

The Orthodox churches have a complex history that continues to influence aspects of the Church's life to this day. It is important that we bear in mind these historical and cultural differences so that we are aware that Orthodoxy is not monolithic, but the lived expression of the Christian hope in particular communities at particular times.

As a religious tradition embedded in different national, geographical and linguistic contexts, there are some culturally distinctive expressions of Orthodoxy. We might think of the unique sound of Georgian Orthodox chant, the painted monasteries of Bucovina, or the Russian custom of diving into icy water on the feast of the Epiphany. Despite these different cultural expressions of Orthodoxy, and the many others besides, the themes of this book reflect universal aspects of Orthodox belief and practice. There is much here, too, that will be familiar or at least have parallels in the Western tradition. Considering them, however, through an Orthodox lens allows us to discover new facets and dimensions of the spiritual life that can enrich our prayer and offer a corrective to the rootlessness, individualism and secularism of our society.

The first chapter will explore the theology and use of icons in Orthodoxy. Icons are usually the first thing people think of in relation to the Orthodox Church, if they think of it at all. They have become a very normal part of our Anglican church furnishing, although we have a less demonstrative relationship to icons than our Orthodox brothers and sisters. Most of us will have seen an icon at some point, whether or not we have ever been inside an Orthodox church. In our screen-dependent age, we can find the static, stony-eyed stares of icons boring or unnerving, preferring the dopamine hit of TV and film. However, the Orthodox understanding of icons can show us how to see icons in a dynamic way that opens our eyes to the spiritual realities at work in our daily lives. Learning to pray with icons can help us to see true reality, with the icons of the saints offering us a window into the Kingdom of God.

The second chapter examines the way that the *Philokalia*, a collection of writings on prayer and the spiritual life, can help us understand ourselves better. This anthology of texts has profoundly shaped Orthodox spirituality. Largely written by monks and for monks, the texts of the *Philokalia* can sometimes seem very austere, but they can also be very *human*. These writings prompt us to take a long, hard look at ourselves; to see what drives us, what tempts us, what our hopes and fears are. Above all, they encourage us to see ourselves as we are meant to be, in our proper relationship to God. We are used to the language of psychoanalysis and therapy, but the *Philokalia* also helps us to understand ourselves in our struggles to grow in faith, hope and love.

The third chapter offers us a way of understanding the celebration of the Eucharist and what it means to live 'liturgically'. The celebration of the Orthodox Liturgy is a profound experience. While there are obviously similarities and parallels to the Western liturgical tradition, the Eastern rite *feels* very different. Many Westerners are drawn by its chant, incense and exoticism. Orthodox theologians of the twentieth century (most notably Fr Alexander Schmemann) put a great emphasis on the Liturgy as the place where we human beings are most fully ourselves and where we see true reality. In our own contexts, we might find the Liturgy repetitious or wordy, far removed from the heavenly wedding banquet! However, with its continual emphasis on the Resurrection, the Orthodox tradition can help us see in our liturgical action a foretaste of the Kingdom made present and visible in the life of the Christian community inside and outside the walls of the church.

In Chapter 4 we will look at the way the Orthodox tradition encourages us to engage with the Scriptures through the lens of Byzantine hymnody. Orthodox hymns are often long and complex, but full of scriptural allusion. Passages of Scripture are put in the mouths of the chanters and congregation, drawing us into the biblical narratives and making them *our* words. Sometimes, whole stories are dramatized poetically, as the motivations and reactions of the characters are reimagined and explored. The Byzantine poet-hymnographers, epitomized by Romanos the Melodist, drew on traditions of poetry that came to the Greek-speaking world from the Syriac-speaking East, through poets and hymnographers such as Ephrem the Syrian. This approach to Scripture is taken up in the works of St Kassiani, the only female Byzantine hymnographer whose works appear in the liturgical books of the Church. Like Romanos, she gives a voice to the voiceless characters of Scripture. Another significant work is the Great Canon of St Andrew of Crete. This is a lengthy hymn on the theme of repentance, which encourages us to learn from the good examples of the Bible and internalize the scriptural story of repentance, mercy and salvation. This tradition of hymn writing shows how the language of Scripture can shape our imaginations and make the biblical story our story.

Last, we will take the image of Divine Light that is so important in Orthodox spirituality and consider the ways the Orthodox tradition can enrich our understanding of the work of the Holy Spirit in the Church and in the world. The Orthodox tradition has a very rich theology of the Holy Spirit, and St Seraphim of Sarov said that to acquire the Holy Spirit is the goal of the Christian life. We might not think of the Orthodox Church as particularly 'Charismatic' or 'Pentecostal', but in reality, it is both! St Symeon the New Theologian and St Seraphim of Sarov had transformative encounters with the Divine Light that show us the way the Holy Spirit extends the saving work of Christ in us, preparing us for the eternal light and glory of the presence of God.

Orthodoxy has much that may seem strange or unfamiliar to us, but there is also much that we have in common. The profound richness of the Orthodox spiritual tradition can help us to see those things more clearly, and there is much that we can learn. It can be easy for us to fixate on the externals, the aesthetics of Orthodoxy. If we can gaze on God, understand ourselves better, live liturgically, make the biblical story our story and bask in the Divine Light, we will discover a vision of the spiritual life that can, in the here and now, transform us more and more into the likeness of Christ.

Notes

1 Pew Research Centre, 2017, 'Orthodox Christianity in the 21st Century', *Pew Research Centre*, 8 November, https://www.pewresearch. org/religion/2017/11/08/orthodox-christianitys-geographic-center-remains-in-central-and-eastern-europe/, accessed 28.05.2025.

2 The systematic killing of Christians in the Near East in 1915 affected Oriental Orthodox communities such as the Armenians and Syrian Orthodox, the Church of the East and, among the Eastern Orthodox, the Pontic Greeks.

I

Icons: Seeing the Saints

The first time that I remember going inside an Orthodox Church, I was in my early teens. It was a church dedicated to my namesake, the Cathedral of St Alexander Nevsky, in Paris.[1] I remember it very vividly: the tall central dome; the way the painted gold walls shone in the light streaming from above; the life-size images of the saints adorning the central columns; the glow of the candle-light. It was quite unlike any other church I had ever been in before. As well as the frescoes on the wall, in every corner and on every free surface stood icons of the saints. Some displayed behind glass, some cased in silver, some even propped up on top of others. Among them, the icons of Jesus and the Virgin Mary were easy to recognize. But there were many others that I couldn't identify, their names inscribed in small Church Slavonic letters, and yet bearing the iconographic signs of sanctity: golden halos, long beards, monastic clothing or episcopal vestments. Our visit was not during a service, so it was relatively quiet; and yet it felt full of people, with so many faces around the church.

For many Anglicans, Roman Catholics and Protestants, it is through icons that they first encounter Orthodoxy. Like me, this may have come about through visiting an Orthodox church for the first time. The number of Orthodox churches in Western Europe has grown significantly in recent years, not least following the accession of Romania and Bulgaria to the European Union in 2007. The opportunities for Western Christians to meet Orthodox congregations have manifestly increased in the last decades, and Orthodox parishes are more and more involved in Churches Together groups in the UK. Many people, however,

7

encounter icons and the Orthodox tradition for the first time in other ways. It is very common to find at least one icon in many Anglican cathedrals and churches, icons of Jesus, Mary or perhaps of the saint of the church's dedication. Similarly, some icons are very well known: we may, for example, have heard a Trinity Sunday sermon exploring Andrei Rublev's famous icon of the Trinity with its three angelic figures seated round a table. Either way, icons with their gold shimmer and penetrative gaze are, for lots of Western Christians, the first way they come to experience Orthodox spirituality.

What is an icon?

We would all recognize an icon if we saw one; they have a very distinctive style. Icon painting is very conservative and there are strong conventions dictating how an icon ought to be painted. As with many traditional art forms, the techniques and methods are passed from teacher to pupil down the generations. Often, famous or miracle-working icons became the template for other depictions of the same saint. For instance, the Prodromiţa icon of the Mother of God (named after the monastic community dedicated to John the Baptist – the Forerunner, 'Prodromos' – on Mount Athos where the icon is found) inspired a much-venerated copy made in 1922 for the monks of the Darvari monastery in Bucharest. There are some small differences between the icons, in the colour of the clothing or in Mary's crown, but they are recognizably the same design. Similarly, the Kazan icon of the Mother of God, according to legend brought from Constantinople to Moscow in the thirteenth century, was very widely copied throughout Russia. Its distinctive iconographic feature is that the Christ-child is standing, presumably on his mother's lap, though this is not visible in the image. The original icon was stolen and (probably) destroyed in 1904 and yet through copies made from the sixteenth century onwards, this particular icon is one of the most important in the Russian religious imagination. We see this continuity of style in all sorts of ways. Icons of the Nativity always show Christ's birth taking place in a rocky cave alongside other elements of the story in the Orthodox tradition, including the midwives (who testify to Christ's ordinary, human birth) or St Joseph and Satan (reflecting an episode in the *Protoevangelium of James* where Joseph is beset with doubts). Likewise, from the Middle East to northern Russia, from the twelfth century until today, St George is depicted on horseback as he spears the dragon below him. One of the reasons that icons are so immediately recognizable to us is because of the continuity of style that goes back through generations of icon painters.

There is, of course, an element of innovation in every generation, and modern production methods have meant that icons can be printed or mass-produced. Understandably, there is some debate about whether or not these are 'proper' icons. In this connection, it may be worth noting that in 2008 a printed copy of the Iveron icon of the Virgin and Child in the Orthodox church in Honolulu, Hawaii, was declared miraculous by the Russian Orthodox Church after it streamed myrrh. Such a miracle would certainly suggest that printed icons were the real thing! Similarly, there have been innovations in iconographic style in recent decades. One of the most refreshing comes from the Orthodox monks on the Isle of Mull, who have developed a style for depicting the Celtic saints. The icons they produce are not strictly 'Byzantine' in style, but are recognizably 'icons' despite some disquiet in certain corners of the internet.

As well as the continuity of style, another aspect that makes an icon stand out from other kinds of religious art is the perspective that is employed. In the West, we are used to a linear perspective: when we look at a painting, we are looking into the distance and the things near us are bigger than the things that are further away. Our eyes are drawn to the so-called 'vanishing point', where parallel lines converge on the horizon. Icons are painted using Byzantine, or inverse, perspective. Here, the 'vanishing point' is not in the distance as the viewer looks at the image. Rather, the 'vanishing point' is in front of the painting.

Byzantine perspective draws the lines and focus of the image towards the viewer rather than away from them. This can lead to some awkward shapes, particularly in examples where Christ is seated on a throne and the throne can sometimes look strangely wide or angular. Nobody really knows why icons are painted like this, and it may be connected to primitive forms of folk-art, but it does mean that the viewer is not passive as they look at the icon; rather, the icon returns the viewer's gaze. The viewer is drawn into the image, becoming themselves part of the icon's focus. This Byzantine perspective is not something we usually encounter in Western art (with the notable exception of Cubist painting)[2] so it stands out to us as another distinctive feature of icon painting.

Why icons?

So, icons are immediately recognizable to us, but why are they so important in the Orthodox tradition? You can't have an Orthodox church without icons: even the smallest, poorest mission chapels will have an icon of the Lord, of the Mother of God and the saint of its dedication. In my experience of Romania, there are icons everywhere: people carry small, laminated icon cards in their wallets and phone cases; when I go to see my doctor, I am greeted by an icon of the holy doctor St Panteleimon; taxi drivers have icons hanging from their rear-view mirrors; you can buy icons, not only in the church-run shops, but at the market where you buy fruit and veg, or anywhere that sells household goods. There is no doubt that icons are an essential part of the belief and practice (and aesthetic imagination) of the Orthodox world.

Theologically speaking, the reason that icons are so important in the Orthodox tradition is to do with the Incarnation, with the fact that God took on our human nature in the person of Jesus Christ. The Russian painter and art historian Leonid Ouspensky wrote that the image is inherent to Christianity because Christianity is 'not only the revelation of the Word of God, but also of the

Image of God, manifested by the God-Man'.[3] At Christmas, we read in the Prologue of St John's Gospel that 'the Word became flesh and lived among us': the *Logos*, the Second Person of the Trinity, the creative, rational principle bringing order out of chaos, became a human being. In the Orthodox tradition, as Ouspensky notes, there is another emphasis. As Christ has come among us as the Word-made-flesh, so too has he come among as the *Image*-made-flesh.

Underlying this view are passages such as Colossians 1.15, 'He is the image of the invisible God', or 2 Corinthians 4.4 where Christ is again described as the 'image of God'. This view is enhanced by the idea in St John's Gospel that anyone who has seen Jesus has seen the Father (see John 12.45 and 14.8–12). In these cases, the Greek word that we translate as 'image' is '*eikon*', from which we get our word 'icon'. Elsewhere in the New Testament *eikon* can mean any kind of image, whether secular (such as the image of Caesar imprinted on a coin in Mark 12.16) or even profane (as with the 'beast and his image' in Revelation 14.11). So it is not a word with a specifically 'holy' meaning, but St Paul uses it to show us that Jesus *reveals* the Father: the image points beyond itself to heavenly realities. It would not be too much of a stretch to translate Colossians 1.15 as 'He [Christ] is the *icon* of the invisible God.'

The defence of icons, rooted in the fact of the Incarnation, was developed by St John of Damascus in the eighth century. His work, *On the Holy Images*, was written in response to a controversy over the use of icons after the Byzantine Emperor Leo III banned them in 730. He uses Scripture to draw the distinction between 'worshipping' created things and 'honouring' created things, demonstrating that icons do not violate the commandment against 'graven images' (Exodus 20.4). John's argument, however, has at its heart the idea that the Incarnation brings human nature (and in fact all created things) into a new communion with the divine nature. He puts it succinctly when he says, 'I do not venerate the creation instead of the creator, but I venerate the Creator, created for my sake, who came down to his creation without being lowered or weakened, that he might glorify my nature.'[4] In the Incarnation, created things can become a channel for God's grace.

A decision in favour of icons was made at the Seventh Ecumenical Council, the Second Council of Nicaea, in 787; though it was raised again by another Emperor Leo (Leo V) in 813, only to finally be resolved in 843 at the Council of Constantinople. This Council is always commemorated on the first Sunday of Lent, known as the 'Triumph of Orthodoxy', where to this day those who 'insult and blaspheme' the holy icons are declared *anathema*.[5] During the periods of state-sanctioned iconoclasm, images were destroyed and replaced with depictions of the cross; monks were forcibly removed from their monasteries; bishops were deposed; and there were even martyrs for the cause of icons. There is some suggestion that the controversy developed in this period because of the rise of aniconic Islam, which caused Christians to rethink their use of images. But this possibility aside, the Jewish roots of Christianity mean that the seeds for this aniconic tendency were planted long before. And, of course, it has resurfaced at various different stages of Christian history, not least in the Protestant Reformation. But after the Council of Constantinople in 843, the issue was settled for the Orthodox world. As Jesus is the *eikon* of the Father, and those who have seen him have seen the Father, so the icons in our churches – as the Second Council of Nicaea affirmed – draw us close to the heavenly realm.

Praying with icons

Icons have a long history in the Eastern Church; they have their own style – almost their own language – and their own theological rationale. But how do we pray with icons? How can they enrich our spiritual lives?

Icons have been a source of fascination for several Western writers. One of the most touching works on the spirituality of icons is *Behold the Beauty of the Lord* by the Dutch Catholic priest Henri Nouwen.[6] Nouwen is well-known for his book on Rembrandt's *The Return of the Prodigal Son* and for his connection with various Christian communities, among them L'Arche.[7] In his book on icons, he offers reflections on four famous images and challenges us to think about how and what we choose to see.

The idea of 'choosing' to see might seem strange. After all, we don't think about seeing; we just open our eyes and take in what is there. But in our age of computer screens, TV screens, social media, billboards and advertisements, what we see *is* a choice and we have agency in what we see. We are very attuned to visual stimuli. On our commutes, it feels easier to scroll through short videos than to sit with our own thoughts (or even to pray); and when we get home, it somehow feels easier to watch TV than to pick up a book. I came across some research that suggests that in the last 20 years, the average time that a person can focus on one thing has dropped from roughly two-and-a-half minutes to only 45 seconds.[8] Our attention is being constantly redirected, by the notifications from our news apps, by social media and by the fact that anything we want to know is only a click away. A lower attention span can affect all sorts of areas of our lives. Undoubtedly the rise in the amount of time we spend on our phones is linked to the decline in the amount of time we spend reading books, but a diminished attention span also affects how we engage with museums and art galleries. In his 2011 Hulsean lecture series, 'The Cost of the Beauty of Holiness', Neil MacGregor related an anecdote in which a Victorian grandee apologized to Holman Hunt because his wife spent *only* 15 minutes looking at his painting, *The Light of the World*.[9] I spent six years as Chaplain of Keble College, Oxford, where the original painting hangs, and I am not sure that even I spent more than 15 minutes looking at it in one go, let alone longer! Perhaps more seriously, our diminished attention spans can make us less alert in our relationships, distracting us in those moments when those closest to us need our support and care. Nevertheless,

Nouwen tells us that 'we do not have to be passive victims of a world that wants to entertain us and distract us.'[10]

Our imaginations, our inner lives, can be shaped by the things we see, the kinds of things we surround ourselves with and which draw our attention. We need only think of the pernicious effects of pornography or violent video games. But it is not just those things that are actively harmful for our souls. When we are distracted, our attention is taken away from the people around us, and from God. So, we need to relearn to pay attention, to 'choose to see' as Nouwen puts it. He says that we must 'safeguard that inner space where we can keep our eyes fixed on the beauty of the Lord'.[11]

As Nouwen describes his encounter with the four icons he explores, he uses the word 'gazing' to express his silent, contemplative seeing. For him, this is the essence of the spirituality of icons. He tells us that, at a difficult time in his life where verbal prayer seemed impossible, it was silently gazing at Rublev's icon of the Trinity that began the process of his healing: 'As I sat for long hours in front of Rublev's Trinity, I noticed how gradually my gaze became a prayer.'[12] And, in a way, these icons took the place of verbal prayer for Nouwen. He says that he memorized them, learnt them by heart, just as he had learnt the Lord's Prayer and the Hail Mary; and so, he could pray with these icons wherever he went.

There is much wisdom here. Prayer can be hard. We can feel overwhelmed, unsure what to say or how to say it. We worry that we are talking into a void or talking to ourselves. When we start to pray, all those distractions from our daily lives can creep up on us. We find that we fill our prayer with those distractions. Some of this can be good, and it is fitting that we bring into God's presence the things that are weighing on our hearts and minds. Some of the distractions, however, are not helpful: our critical inner voices, our rumbling stomachs or our wondering what we should be doing next. We have a natural tendency to try and fill silence.

Praying with icons can help us overcome some of these barriers to prayer. We are reminded that prayer is not an intellectual activity: as we strike a match, with its distinctive sound and smell, to light a candle; as the flame flickers and the gold of the icon glows in the candlelight; perhaps as we make the sign of the Cross over our bodies; and as we breathe deeply. In this preparatory action, we are led away from the busyness of our ordinary lives and into the present moment. God's grace comes to us in these material things, just as God has come among us in the Incarnation. We find that our eyes move across the icon, noticing details, perhaps not yet ready to look into the eyes of the Lord or of the saint depicted. We notice the unusual perspective, the objects, the posture and the colours. And slowly our gaze is fixed, and we find that we can pray. Icons can help us to keep our focus, drawing our mind back when we are distracted, and inviting us to see anew with the eye of our hearts.

The gaze of God

As we relearn to fix our gaze, we discover that there is a reciprocity in gazing. As we look on the image in an icon, we discover that we are being looked upon by the loving eyes of the Lord and his saints. The Byzantine perspective of an icon makes us the focal point, makes us part of the image. We cannot be casual observers, casting an eye over an icon. We stand at the 'vanishing point' and so the icon looks at us. We might find this unnerving, particularly given the fixed stare of a still image. But God looks on us with the love that drew us into existence and sustains our every moment. To be seen by God is to be known intimately, better than we know ourselves, and to be loved beyond measure. To be looked upon by God is transformative. The journal of the martyr-monk Christophe Lebreton, one of the seven Trappist monks killed in Algeria in 1996, carries the title *Born from the Gaze of God*.[13] It is such an evocative phrase and one that comes to me often. The gaze of God is life-giving, even in the midst of suffering and death. Through God's gaze, we know his closeness to us, seeing his work in ourselves and in the lives of the saints. The epilogue of Andrei Tarkovsky's 1966 film *Andrei Rublev* presents a montage of details from Rublev's icons. It is the only part of the three-hour film that is in colour, so it is visually striking. The last part of the sequence shows a close-up of Christ's eyes in Rublev's icon Christ the Redeemer, as the camera slowly draws away revealing Christ's face.[14] It is an impressive piece of cinema, but gives a powerful sense of being seen by the icon of Christ.

Looking at an icon becomes a moment of encounter, once we have shed all the distractions that hold us back from God. At first glance, the rigid posture and the stern faces of the Byzantine style might seem profoundly impersonal, but the more time we spend in their company, in contemplation of them, their features seem less harsh and more inviting. It is not that the expressions of the icons have changed, but that we have been changed by the loving gaze of God. It is not their faces that have softened, but our hearts. Through our prayer before the icon, we become ready to come face-to-face with the Living God and, like Moses, to speak to him as a friend (Exodus 33.11).

Shaping our imaginations

If we can keep our eyes fixed on the beauty of the Lord, to return to Henri Nouwen's phrase, we can know God's presence with us, and we can actively choose to see God's reality breaking through into the humdrum of our every day. We can say 'yes' to the invitation that an icon sets before us, drawing us into the story of our salvation.

Nouwen referred to memorizing an icon, seeing them whether or not they are physically present. In a way, I think that's quite natural: the objects and images we see every day, or that have strong emotional connections for us, can imprint themselves very strongly on our memories. And being able to visualize an icon that has meant something to us through our prayer can be a helpful way of praying, even when we don't have the icon with us. I think, however, that this would sound quite strange in an Orthodox context. I've mentioned already how omnipresent icons are in Orthodox societies, and icons are made in all shapes and sizes precisely so that we can have access to them wherever we are and whatever we are doing. No matter whether it's a small travel-sized diptych of our Lord and the Virgin Mary, or a favourite icon at home or at church, there is no substitute for the real thing!

This omnipresence can profoundly affect our imaginations and our spiritual life. If we have icons in our homes, our cars, our workplaces, our pockets even, then we cannot help but be shaped by the spirituality of icons. It is common for Orthodox households to have an icon of the Last Supper in the kitchen, for instance, and so every time a meal is prepared, there is an evocation of that particular meal and its place in the biblical story. Likewise, if I have a small icon card in my phone case, whenever I get my phone out, the saint's image briefly invites me to attend to their presence and to ask their intercession. I'm not sure that my family would agree, but you can never have too many icons! They break down our rigid separation of the Church and the rest of life, the sacred and the secular, as our homes become little churches. And they show us God's power to change our lives, just as he was at work in the lives of the saints. I have a beautiful icon of St Alexander Nevsky that was given to me on the tenth anniversary of my ordination to the priesthood. It sits on my mantelpiece and every day, as I see it, I am reminded that if God can sanctify the life of a thirteenth-century Russian warlord, he can sanctify my life too!

The contemplation of icons that Henri Nouwen describes, the silent gazing on them and the experience of the gaze of God, is a valuable kind of prayer. Icons can call us to attend to spiritual things in the middle of our daily lives, and they form our habits of prayer and devotion. In all the distractions we face on our phones, computers and TVs, the icon can make us stop, be still, and see and attend to the presence of God with us.

The dynamic power of icons

That said, there is another, more dynamic, aspect to the spirituality of icons that I would like us to explore. It doesn't undermine the contemplative vision that many Western writers on icons present, but it is a facet of the spirituality that is evident in the lived experience of Orthodox Christians.

Given the ways in which we are bombarded with moving images in all sorts of different areas of our lives, and the dopamine hit we get from TV and social media, we might find the static, staring iconography of the Byzantine style unnerving, or even boring. But icons always tell a story. An icon of the Annunciation is a snapshot of a moment in our salvation history. We see the Archangel Gabriel on one side of the image and Mary on the other. Gabriel's hand is raised as he announces the news to Mary that she will bear a son. A beam of light usually travels, sometimes with the small image of a dove, from the top-centre of the icon, touching Mary. In this freeze-frame image, we are drawn into the action and the emotion of the biblical scene. Some icons, usually of biblical scenes but also of the lives of the saints, compress different elements of the story into the one image. Initially, this can be a bit confusing until you have worked out what is going on. I referred earlier to the way that different elements of the Nativity story are usually presented in the icons of Jesus' birth, but it is easy to see in other examples too. An icon of St Elijah, being whisked to heaven in the fiery chariot, may also depict Elisha striking the waters with Elijah's mantle (which happens afterwards) and a smaller image of Elijah in a cave receiving food from the ravens (which happens beforehand in the story of Elijah). In one sense, this is a limitation of the medium: you can't otherwise paint the past, present and future at the same time. But I think there is a more profound reason for this. As depictions of sacred events, related biblical scenes can appear concurrently, inviting us to see the narrative as a whole. There is a kind of icon that depicts the 12 major feasts of the Church all on the same icon.[15] The theological justification for this is clear: the saving events of the life, death and Resurrection of Jesus Christ are not events in linear time, but in sacred time.

One of my favourite icons, though only a print mounted on wood, is an icon I have of Moses and the Burning Bush. In the middle of the Burning Bush, with small flames licking its branches, is the Virgin Mary holding the Christ-child. The Burning Bush (or in Orthodoxy, the Unburnt Bush) is understood as a type of Mary, set aflame by the Holy Spirit, giving birth while remaining a virgin.[16] An angel appears from behind the bush, hand extended towards the figure of Moses at the left side of the icon, who looks up at the angel, arms raised in answer. Between the standing figure of Moses on the left and the Burning Bush on the right, crouched close to the ground, Moses appears a second time. Here, he is untying his sandals in response to the angelic words, 'Come no closer! Remove the sandals from your feet, for the place on which you are standing is holy ground' (Exodus 3.5). There is so much movement in this simple composition as we 'read' it from left to right, that the viewer cannot but feel the dynamism of the narrative scene.

As well as the dynamism and movement we can see in the icons themselves, it is also worth reflecting on how icons are used. If we take Henri Nouwen as our sole guide, we might imagine a constant, peaceful, quiet contemplation of icons in church and home. My experience in the Orthodox world is very different! People engage with icons in all sorts of dynamic ways. As Orthodox Christians approach to venerate icons in church, they bow low and make the sign of the Cross three times before they kiss the icon. Icons are carried in church processions, or even at political protests! I have seen people press photos of their loved ones against the icons or frescoes in church, or tuck small slips of paper with their prayer requests into the frames. This is yet another reminder that icons are small, tangible signs of the grace of God made present in creation.

Icons: helping us to see

We have explored the contemplative and dynamic aspects of the spirituality of icons. Western writers, like Henri Nouwen, have often emphasized the silent gazing of our prayer in the presence of an icon, but this is not the whole picture: the movement and action inherent in the icons themselves, and in our veneration of them, show the power of Orthodox spirituality to make holiness a part of our everyday lives.

Above all, the Orthodox veneration of icons challenges us to relearn how to see. The images of the Lord and his saints call us to notice their presence in our daily lives, and to pay attention to our place in salvation history. Through both the silent gazing that Nouwen describes, and also through our active engagement with icons as material channels of God's grace, we can relearn to see the ways in which God is working in us and through us. Holiness is not just for the saints we depict on the walls of our churches; holiness is our vocation, our calling too. The veneration of icons helps us to put away the myriad distractions we see all around us and which we face day to day. Through them, like windows into the Kingdom, we see the Lord's love and goodness shining on us.

We are changed by our veneration of icons. Our hearts are softened, our eyes are opened, and we become more attentive to God's presence. In a way, we *become* icons. We become images of the Love that has been poured out upon us. As Christ is the image, the *eikon*, of God, we are destined to become images, *eikones*, of Christ. St Paul tells us that 'Just as we have borne the image of the man of dust, we will also bear the image of the man of heaven' (1 Corinthians 15.49). Our earthly existence is contrasted with our final destiny as those who bear the image of Christ. But this isn't just something we await at the Resurrection on the Last Day. Rather, it begins now: 'And all of us, with unveiled faces, seeing the glory of the Lord as though reflected in a mirror, are being transformed into the same image [the same *eikon*] from one degree of glory to another' (2 Corinthians 3.18).

Through God's immeasurable love for us, we can become living icons of Christ and signs of his grace at work in our lives.

Notes

1 The Cathedral of Saint Alexander Nevsky in Paris was established with the support of Tsar Alexander II in 1861.

2 See, for instance, Picasso's 1909 painting, *The Reservoir, Horta de Ebro*.

3 Leonid Ouspensky, 1992, *Theology of the Icon*, vol. 1, New York: SVS Press, p. 4.

4 Andrew Louth, trans., 2003, *John of Damascus: Three Treatises on the Divine Images*, New York: SVS Press, p. 22.

5 'The Synodikon of Orthodoxy', n.d., https://roea.org/files/Liturgic al-Texts/The-Synodikon-of-Orthodoxy-I.pdf, accessed 13.09.2024.

6 Henri Nouwen, 1987, *Behold the Beauty of the Lord: Praying with Icons*, Notre Dame, IN: Ave Maria Press.

7 Henri Nouwen, 1992, *The Return of the Prodigal Son: A Story of Homecoming*, London: Darton, Longman and Todd.

8 Northeastern Global News, 2024, 'Squirrel! Why Attention Spans Seem to be Shrinking and What We Can Do about It', 23 January, https://news.northeastern.edu/2024/01/23/decreasing-attention-span, accessed 13.09.2024.

9 I am grateful to Revd Dr James Gardom for this anecdote.

10 Nouwen, *Behold the Beauty of the Lord*, p. 12.

11 Nouwen, *Behold the Beauty of the Lord*, p. 12.

12 Nouwen, *Behold the Beauty of the Lord*, p. 21.

13 Christophe Lebreton, 2014, *Born from the Gaze of God: The Tibhirine Journal of a Martyr Monk (1993–1996)*, Collegeville, PA: Cistercian Publications.

14 Painted some time in the 1420s, and rediscovered by accident in 1919, Rublev's icon of Christ the Redeemer is now displayed in Moscow's Tretyakov Gallery. I am grateful to Revd Dr Arabella Milbank Robinson for this observation.

15 The Orthodox liturgical year begins in September, and so the order of the Twelve Great Feasts runs: the Nativity of the Theotokos; the Exaltation of the Cross; the Presentation of the Theotokos; the Nativity of Christ; the Baptism of Christ; the Presentation of Jesus in the Temple; the Annunciation; the Entry into Jerusalem; the Ascension of Christ; Pentecost; the Transfiguration of Jesus; and the Dormition of the Theotokos.

Note that Easter, considered the Feast of Feasts, is considered separately as the greatest of all holy days.

16 As seen in one of the hymns for the feast of the 'Unburnt Bush' Icon of the Mother of God: 'You showed Moses, O Christ God, an image of your most pure Mother in the bush that burned yet was not consumed, for she herself was not consumed, when she received in her womb the fire of divinity! She remained incorrupt after her pure childbearing! By her prayers, O greatly merciful One, deliver us from the flame of passions, and preserve your people from all harm!' Orthodox Church in America, '"Unburnt Bush" Icon of the Mother of God – Troparion & Kontakion', https://www.oca.org/saints/troparia/2012/09/04/102500-unburnt-bush-icon-of-the-mother-of-god, accessed 13.09.2024. This typology also provides the title for Sergius Bulgakov's work on Mary: Sergius Bulgakov, 2009, *The Burning Bush: On the Orthodox Veneration of the Mother of God*, Grand Rapids, MI: William B. Eerdmans Publishing Company. For more on the 'passions', see Chapter 2 on the *Philokalia*.

2

The *Philokalia*: Seeing Ourselves

One Advent, a few years ago, I set myself the challenge of reading all four volumes of the English translation of the *Philokalia*.[1] I did not succeed. Since then, the fifth and final volume has been published, so there's more to read than when I started. I realize now that I was approaching the text in completely the wrong way, as if I had decided to read the Bible from cover to cover and opened it at the first page of Genesis.

The *Philokalia*, like the Bible, is a compilation of texts written by different people over hundreds of years, from the fourth century to the fifteenth century. These various writings (which are largely about prayer) were brought together by two monks of Mount Athos, Nicodemus and Macarius, and published for the first time (in Greek) in 1782. The title, '*Philokalia*', means 'love of the beautiful', pointing to the spiritual beauty of the texts contained within it. As an indication of this spiritual beauty, the translators of the English version describe it thus:

> The *Philokalia* is an itinerary through the labyrinth of time, a silent way of love and gnosis through the deserts and emptiness of life, especially modern life, a vivifying and fadeless presence ... It is a summons to [man] to overcome his ignorance, to uncover the knowledge that lies within, to rid himself of illusion, and to be receptive to the grace of the Holy Spirit who teaches all things.[2]

Selections of it were translated into Church Slavonic by St Paisius Velichkovsky very soon after the first edition appeared, in 1793.

23

Early translations were made into Russian, and from there, into a host of modern languages.[3] Despite its relative newness (not yet 250 years have passed since its publication, and that is not long in Orthodoxy!), it achieved an extraordinary popularity. In the beautiful nineteenth-century tale, *The Way of a Pilgrim*, the *Philokalia* is the book that the unnamed Russian pilgrim carries with him in his efforts to understand the Scripture, 'pray without ceasing' (1 Thessalonians 5.16).[4] Dostoevsky had a deep connection to Optina monastery where the teachings of the *Philokalia* were put into practice: through the figure of Elder Zosima in *The Brothers Karamazov*, the spirituality of the *Philokalia* has come to a wide audience.[5] The writings on prayer contained in the *Philokalia* have had a profound influence on the development of Orthodox spirituality in the last two centuries: Andrew Louth describes its publication in 1782 as 'a watershed moment in the history of Orthodox theology'.[6]

Where did the *Philokalia* come from?

This 'watershed moment' didn't come from thin air. Rather, its background lies in a time of spiritual renewal on Mount Athos, the 'Holy Mountain', during the second half of the eighteenth century. In 1754, a dispute arose in one of the monastic communities about whether the memorial services for the dead could be offered on a Sunday. On the one hand, some of the monks maintained that the day of the Resurrection was a fitting time for the commemoration of the departed. On the other hand, others held that Saturday was the usual day for these commemorations and there was no good reason to depart from this practice. As with many things in the life of the Church, the real issue at stake was not the particular point of contention (a matter of liturgical scheduling), but deeper questions about the relationship to tradition and the inheritance of the faith.[7] The monks that opposed the innovation became known as the *Kollyvades*, a name derived from the cakes of boiled wheat (*kollyva*) used in the memorial services, but far from being a single-issue movement, they also advocated a return to traditional practices of prayer and the frequent reception of Holy Communion. The dispute on Mount Athos was bitter and lasted for decades. The leaders of the *Kollyvades* movement were condemned by the Synod of Constantinople in 1776, though this decision was overturned following an appeal in 1781. It was in the following year that the first edition of the *Philokalia* appeared. It may seem like an inauspicious start to a movement of spiritual renewal, but the intense period of debate allowed the *Kollyvades* to scour the patristic literature to demonstrate the truth of their arguments. They maintained that the practices they upheld were part of an unchanging Orthodox tradition. The extensive writings of St Nicodemus, one of the two monks who compiled the *Philokalia*, are completely full of references to the Church Fathers.[8] It is in this context that the *Philokalia* was published. The various writings that the *Philokalia* contains were selected specifically to show the value of prayer. But the *Kollyvades* were not just interested in prayer in general. Rather, the movement of spiritual renewal on Mount Athos emphasized 'hesychastic' prayer (from the Greek word for stillness) and which was called by St Nicodemus the 'prayer of the heart'.[9]

The Jesus Prayer

You may have heard of the 'Jesus Prayer'. As with icons, this is an aspect of Orthodox spirituality that has been explored by Christians in other church traditions in recent years.[10] In essence, a short form of words is used repetitively to still our minds, slow our breathing and make us attentive to the presence of God. This has led to descriptions of the Jesus Prayer as a kind of 'Christian mindfulness', which goes some way to explain its contemporary popularity and resonance. The prayer is simple: 'Lord Jesus Christ, Son of God, have mercy on me.' It is a prayer that says something about who Jesus is (that he is Lord and God) and something about who we are (sinners in need of mercy). This prayer thus contains a profound spiritual richness and helps us to see who we are and who God is, a theme from the *Philokalia* to which we will return.

The precise form of words can vary. Sometimes, the prayer is given as 'Lord Jesus Christ, Son of God, have mercy on me, a sinner.' In other contexts, particularly when it is said corporately, it might be recited as 'Lord Jesus Christ, Son of God, have mercy on us.' Some people have told me that if they are using the Jesus Prayer in their intercessions, they include the people for whom they are praying: 'Lord Jesus Christ, Son of God, have mercy on *x*.' Similarly, the prayer is sometimes said or sometimes sung. It also has a different intonation in different languages. Some people like to use a knotted prayer rope or beads as part of the meditative repetition, but this is not essential. These variations are worth experimenting with; I have found my prayer life enriched by them at different times.

It is in the constant repetition of the Jesus Prayer that the anonymous Russian pilgrim finds an understanding of what it means to 'pray without ceasing'. He meets a monk who tells him,

> One who accustoms himself to this appeal experiences as a result so deep a consolation and so great a need to offer the prayer always, that he can no longer live without it, and it will continue to voice itself within him of its own accord.[11]

This simple recollection can become for us like breathing or even a heartbeat, something that we are not always aware of, but which keeps us going. It is a prayer for walking the dog or washing up, a preparation for our work or important events. It is a prayer for when we wake up and for when we are tossing and turning in the middle of the night. The Jesus Prayer makes us attentive to God's presence in all the busyness and distractions of our daily lives. 'Lord Jesus Christ, Son of God, have mercy on me.'

It is a prayer that is beautiful in its simplicity. We might be surprised that this short prayer is the key to the spiritual heights to which many saints have aspired. But our faith is not a gnostic religion; there is no secret knowledge in Christianity. The path to the profound experience of prayer, of nearness to God, is laid plainly before us. The Jesus Prayer is not just for monks in their monasteries, but for all Christians. As the pilgrim finds in *The Way of a Pilgrim*, it takes time and practice, but it is a way of prayer that we can all learn. It can become part of our internal rhythm, like our breath and our heartbeat, as we constantly call on the name of Jesus from the very depths of our being.

While a lot of the Western literature on the Jesus Prayer points to the radical transformation it can bring to our personal prayer, there is also a long tradition of using the Jesus Prayer corporately in the Orthodox tradition. To be an individual, a human being dependent on God's mercy, in proper relation to God, is to stand alongside our brothers and sisters, who also call on the Lord's name. The first time I experienced this was at a monastic service of vespers in Bucharest. I had turned up for evening prayer one Sunday and took my place in the crowded church. The lights were dim and the service began with a solitary monk reciting the Jesus Prayer in the centre of the church. This went on for quite some time, and eventually another monk replaced him. I thought this would mark the start of vespers, but instead, this second monk just took over the recitation of the Jesus Prayer. Altogether, I think there were 40 minutes of the Jesus Prayer said aloud by a single voice, and silently, lips moving among the congregation, before vespers began. Afterwards, a monk asked how I found it, explaining that this was how it was done on Mount Athos. At the Orthodox monastery of St John the Baptist in Essex, the Jesus Prayer is said in the church for two hours every morning and two hours every evening. The founder of the monastery, St Sophrony of Essex, was a disciple of St Silouan of Mount Athos, and he wrote extensively and beautifully on the Jesus Prayer.[12] This serves to remind us that even with those prayer practices we think of as 'private prayer' we never pray alone. Rather, 'we are very members incorporate in the mystical body of thy Son, which is the blessed company of all faithful people', as the Book of Common Prayer puts it.[13] The relationship between the corporate, liturgical prayer and the Jesus Prayer is further seen in the fact that in some Orthodox traditions, the saying of the daily services can be replaced by the recitation of the Jesus Prayer a particular number of times if a monk (or indeed a layman) does not have access to the necessary liturgical texts.[14]

The Jesus Prayer, the 'prayer of the heart', is one of the profound treasures of the Orthodox tradition and it has shaped Orthodox spirituality since the spiritual renewal that began on Mount Athos in the eighteenth century. For many Anglicans, Roman Catholics and Protestants, the Jesus Prayer is the first point of contact with the tradition of hesychasm – the search for *hesychia*, stillness – which the *Philokalia* expounds.

The prayer of the heart and the *Philokalia*

So, what does the *Philokalia* have to say about the prayer of the heart? In some ways, that is a difficult question to answer as the five volumes of the English translation run to almost 2,000 pages! While the different authors have their own styles of writing, the texts often point to the same spiritual truths or give the same advice. It is easy to lose track of whether a particular quotation comes from St Mark the Ascetic in the fifth century or from Nikitas Stithatos in the eleventh.[15] And because the texts come from such a wide historical timeframe, the later writers knew the works of the earlier writers, whom they quote and whose teachings they pass on. This means that reading the *Philokalia* is an immersive experience, and the repetition in the texts is almost like an act of hesychastic prayer in itself. The lessons of the *Philokalia* are reinforced with every new text, drawing us upwards in a spiral towards a deeper understanding of the spiritual life.

Some of the texts on prayer are extremely hands-on, coming from a lifetime of monastic experience. For instance, there is a text by St Gregory of Sinai, *On Prayer*, made up of seven short sections.[16] The first tackles the very practical question of how to sit while praying the Jesus Prayer. He recommends sitting on a stool, but recognizes that if this becomes too hard after a while, it is a good idea to sit on a mattress. St Gregory also, no doubt speaking from experience, says that we should not get up too quickly if we are feeling discouraged or distracted, but patiently focus on our prayer. Another example of this practical advice can be seen in a text attributed to St Symeon the New Theologian.[17] Here, we are advised not to look upwards or raise our hands aloft, but to sit quietly and close the door. 'Rest your beard on your chest [for those who have them!] and focus your physical gaze ... upon the centre of your belly or your navel.'[18] Our breathing should not be through the nose, but through the mouth in order to make us more conscious of it and thus aid our prayer.

Other texts of the *Philokalia* provide us with beautiful descriptions of the experience of prayer. St Diadochos of Photiki, for example, writes in his *On Spiritual Knowledge and Discrimination*,

> Sometimes the soul is kindled into love for God and, free from all fantasy and image, moves untroubled by doubt towards Him; and it draws, as it were, the body with it into the depths of that ineffable love ... The soul is aware of nothing except what it is moving towards. When we experience things in this manner, we can be sure that it is the energy of the Holy Spirit within us.[19]

Such texts inspire us to continue in the pursuit of the prayer of the heart and not give up when things seem difficult, holding before us the experience of communion with God for which we long.

Among the writings we find in the *Philokalia* are also compilations of short texts, usually grouped into 'centuries' (that is, a hundred sayings on a particular theme). In St Symeon the New Theologian's *One Hundred and Fifty-Three Practical and*

Theological Texts, for instance, we find the following example: 'Earth thrown on a fire puts it out. Similarly, worldly concerns and attachment to even the smallest and insignificant thing quell the fervour initially burning in our hearts.'[20] These pieces of wisdom can provide excellent food for thought, giving us advice for prayer and the spiritual life, and they are often striking in their imagery.

There is also a great emphasis on the love of God and of our neighbours in these texts. Selections from the writing of St Maximos the Confessor make up a substantial part of the second volume of the *Philokalia*, and one of these is entitled *Four Hundred Texts on Love*.[21] Right at the beginning, St Maximos tells us that love is not just a warm, fuzzy feeling but 'a holy state of the soul'. Achieving this state is the goal of the spiritual life and is related to how we think and act, in relation to ourselves and to others. Love is practical. 'The state of love may be recognized in the giving of money, and still more in the giving of spiritual counsel and looking after people in their physical needs.'[22] Our dependence on one another in our search for union with God is beautifully described by St Thalassios the Libyan: 'An all-embracing and intense longing for God binds those who experience it both to God and to one another ... Love alone harmoniously joins all created things with God and with each other.'[23] We find in the texts of the *Philokalia* a clear sense that love is transformative, drawing us closer to God and to each other.

For the writers of the texts included in the *Philokalia*, prayer is a way of learning to love and entering into communion with the God who loves us. Prayer, and specifically hesychastic prayer (the prayer of the heart) is a way of uniting our hearts and minds. In the language of the *Philokalia*, our intellects are drawn down into our hearts by prayer.[24] Nikiphoros the Monk illustrates this beautifully when he writes,

You know that what we breathe is air. When we exhale it, it is for the heart's sake, for the heart is the source of life and warmth for the body. The heart draws towards itself the air inhaled when breathing ... Seat yourself, then, concentrate your intellect, and lead it into the respiratory passages through which your breath passes into your heart ... Once it has entered there, what follows will be neither dismal nor glum. Just as a man, after being far away from home, on his return is over-joyed at being with his wife and children again, so the intellect, once it is united with the soul, is filled with indescribable de-light ... When your intellect is firmly established in your heart, it must not remain idle and silent; it should constantly repeat and meditate on the prayer 'Lord Jesus Christ, Son of God, have mercy on me.'[25]

Aside from some questionable biology from a modern point of view, Nikiphoros' description expresses the essence of hesy-chastic prayer: through our breathing, and through the slow repetition of the Jesus Prayer, our hearts and minds can find unity, stillness and the presence of God. The search for *hesychia* is not a search beyond ourselves: we do not find it in the created world or even in the liturgical worship of the Church. *Hesychia* is found within us. It is because of this fundamental conviction that the *Philokalia* has a rich vocabulary for what we would now call psychoanalysis. The search for stillness within ourselves requires us to understand ourselves better, our instincts, motiva-tions, desires. The writers of the texts of the *Philokalia* encourage us to know what is going on in our innermost selves so that we can disentangle the good from the bad, working to free ourselves from the things that hold us back from God.

Seeing ourselves more clearly

At the heart of the kind of prayer conceived of in the *Philokalia* is a vision of the human person created and loved by God. In his book, *Looking East in Winter*, Rowan Williams writes,

The teaching of the *Philokalia* presupposes a many-layered analysis of human consciousness at the centre of which lies a very particular reading of the meaning of the image of God in us. It is an anthropology that goes far deeper than the conventional assumptions so often made by Christians and non-Christians alike about the division of body and soul ... and in positing a fundamental unity of perception of what is lost in the Fall, it challenges all fragmented accounts of human knowing and sensing ... Restored humanity is humanity properly embodied, and this embodiment includes the freedom to relate to the things and the persons of the world as they are in relation to God.[26]

Despite what we might think about monastic attitudes to the body, the *Philokalia* in fact invites us to understand our bodies, our emotions, our senses, as aids to the union with God for which we long.

But clearly, things are not as they should be. In our fallen, human weakness, our bodies, our emotions and our senses can draw us away from God, just as easily as they can lead us to him. We lash out in anger; overindulge from greed; pursue our sexual desire or our desire for power and control. There is a long tradition, stretching back into the world of Greek philosophy, of seeing the senses as windows through which evil can enter the soul: thus we must be self-disciplined and show mastery over the body.[27] Such a view is inherited by the Christian tradition through the Jewish writer Philo, and it is abundantly evident, even as early as the second century, in the work of Clement of Alexandria.[28]

It is in this context that the *Philokalia* presents us with a rich vocabulary for understanding our thoughts, impulses and actions. The writings contained within the *Philokalia* call us to a radical kind of honesty, about ourselves, about our relationships with each other and with God. But this is no easy task. We like to be comfortable. We subconsciously mask our innermost selves. In order to achieve this radical honesty, we must slowly peel back the layers of our self-delusion and identify those things within ourselves that cause us to sin.

To assist us in this task, we find within the *Philokalia* the language of the 'passions' (*pathē* in Greek). These are the impulses that emerge within our souls and cause us to think or act in a certain way. There are various lists of the passions in the different writings of the *Philokalia*: St Peter of Damaskos has a list of 298 passions, which he identifies from Scripture, beginning with 'harshness, trickery, malice, perversity, mindlessness' and so on. Evagrios and St John Cassian give us the eight 'evil thoughts' (*logismoi*), which in Western Christianity become the Seven Deadly Sins.[29]

But it is important to note that the experience of the 'passions' is not the same as sin. In the lists of the passions that we find in the *Philokalia*, we are not given a checklist of sins but a way of understanding how our impulses – not inherently sinful – lead us into thoughts and actions that distance us from God and our neighbours. The passions happen to us, they are experienced passively, and it is our entertaining them in thought, or our enacting them, that is sinful. It is not a sin to be hungry or to experience sexual desire, for instance; but it becomes so when we allow these impulses to drive us to greed or lust, allowing the passions to take control within us.

St John of Damaskos tells us that the soul has three parts (an idea inherited from Plato): the intelligent, reasonable part; the incensive, inflammatory part; and the desiring part. Each part can cause us to sin in particular ways. The intelligent part can provoke us to folly or ingratitude; the incensive to anger or envy; the desiring to greed or unchastity.[30] Through the practice of the corresponding virtues, these passions within our souls can be trained, rebalancing our souls, bringing us to a state of *apatheia*, 'passionlessness' (which is not the same as 'apathy' in modern English use!). But in order to do this, we need to look deep within ourselves and identify those passions to which we are particularly susceptible. St Isaiah the Solitary writes: 'Examine yourself daily in the sight of God, and discover which of the passions is in your heart … Be attentive to yourself.'[31] There is no 'one size fits all' approach to the passions. Each of us will struggle with different things in different ways. Some of the writings in the *Philokalia* might seem harsh, but there is also a deep compassion that comes from understanding the way we struggle with sin. St Theodoros, for instance, tells us: 'do not revile your brother for his faults, lest you lapse from kindness and love.'[32] If we can be honest with ourselves (and God) about those things that tempt or distract us, we can begin a process of self-transformation, weeding out those things that hold us back from God. Rowan Williams notes that as we learn to see ourselves properly, understanding the positive and negative impulses at work within us, we come to realize God's *apatheia* towards us:

> God does not see us reactively; God is not roused to fury and disgust by the sight of us – nor is God persuaded to love us because we are successful. God sees what is there, embraces it in His love and transforms it in His grace – the essence of the Gospel of Jesus Christ.[33]

The writings of the *Philokalia* call us to see ourselves differently. We must be aware of our weaknesses, trust in God's mercy and know that we are loved beyond all measure.

The radical honesty required by this process of transformation shines a light into the deepest parts of our being, and it may be uncomfortable, surprising or unnerving. This is why the *Philokalia* speaks so often about having a spiritual guide, a 'spiritual father' in the language of these texts. St Symeon the New Theologian often writes about the importance of a spiritual father. In a text called *On Faith*, he tells the story of a young man who drifts back into his worldly life after a mystical experience because he ignored the advice of his spiritual father. It is only when he returns to the 'saintly elder' with contrition and obedience that he again finds the grace he encountered in his youth.[34] The significance of this relationship is an important part of Orthodox spirituality, revived in modern times by the influence of the *Philokalia* and the spiritual elders (*startsy*) of early nineteenth-century Russia.[35]

A relationship such as this requires a great deal of trust, but a good spiritual director will be able to ensure we are being genuinely honest with ourselves and also prevent us from despairing at our own sinfulness. In the Anglican tradition, clergy are generally expected to have a spiritual director, but it is something from which every Christian can benefit. Many Orthodox Christians have a 'spiritual father' whom they consult before making important decisions and who can give direction in their spiritual lives. Most dioceses have a list of trained spiritual directors available and talking with your parish priest is often a good start.

Learning to be honest requires humility. We have to face up to ourselves as we really are, with all the weaknesses of our fallen humanity. Ilias the Presbyter uses the striking image of a merchant with his gold. He says that a merchant without gold is no merchant at all and the one who aspires to the spiritual life, but who does not have the gold of humility, will never possess the joy of virtue.[36] Humility is an essential part of the process of self-transformation to which we are called. St Peter of Damaskos even goes so far as to say that humility is necessary for our salvation.[37] But humility is not just about recognizing our own sinfulness. The radical honesty of the spiritual life requires us to see who we are in relation to God. We have to recognize our complete and utter dependence on the God who created us, loves us and sustains our existence. Humility should not lead us down a spiral of self-doubt and dejection. Rather, humility frees us to see things as God sees them. Peter writes:

Even if you are not what you should be, you should not despair. It is bad enough that you have sinned; why in addition do you wrong God by regarding him in your ignorance as powerless? Is he, who for your sake created the great universe that you behold, incapable of saving your soul?[38]

God is always acting for our good, and as Peter says a little later in this passage, humility will cause us to 'marvel at God's compassion'.[39] The *Philokalia* asks us to understand ourselves better, to be aware of the impulses and desires at work in us, and to see the grace and mercy of God drawing us out of our self-deception into the abundant life that God has promised us.

Taking up the invitation

Coming from a moment of spiritual renewal 250 years ago, the *Philokalia* had a profound impact on the development of Orthodox spirituality, and it continues to be a rich resource for our spiritual lives.

The *Philokalia* contains immeasurable wisdom on the practicalities of prayer, encouraging us always to persist and looking on our failings with compassion. We are to use all of ourselves, our minds, hearts and our bodies in prayer. For the writers of these texts, prayer is like our breathing, unnoticed and life-sustaining, and our breathing too can help us to pray. The Jesus Prayer, the prayer of the heart, is one of the greatest gifts of this spiritual tradition, beautiful in its simplicity and full of hidden depths: 'Lord Jesus Christ, Son of God, have mercy on me.'

This fundamental recognition of our need for God's mercy also means that the *Philokalia* gives us a grammar and a vocabulary to see and understand what is going on inside of us, in the depths of our souls. By attending to the passions working in us, we can loosen their grip on us, countering sin with virtue, but always trusting in God's goodness and love. Above all, the *Philokalia* invites us to see ourselves as God sees us. If we can develop this radical honesty about ourselves and our human nature, we can see where God is at work. Thus, we can come closer to the union with God that is the deepest longing of our souls.

Notes

1 Gerald Palmer, Kallistos Ware and Philip Sherrard, trans., 1979–2024, *The Philokalia: The Complete Text*, vols. 1–5, London: Faber and Faber.

2 Palmer, Ware and Sherrard, trans., *The Philokalia*, vol. 1, pp. 13–14.

3 As new editions and translations were produced, often additional texts were added to the original compilation. The Romanian edition, prepared by Fr (now St) Dumitru Stăniloae, runs to 12 volumes.

4 Reginald Michael French, trans., 1995, *The Way of a Pilgrim: A Classic of Orthodox Spirituality*, London: SPCK.

5 Nel Grillaert, 2011, '"Raise the People in Silence": Traces of Hesychasm in Dostoevskij's Fictional Saint Zosima', *Dostoevsky Studies*, New Series, 15, pp. 47–88.

6 Andrew Louth, 2015, *Modern Orthodox Thinkers: From the Philokalia to the Present*, London: SPCK, p. 1.

7 It is worth remembering that the theological debates on Mount Athos were (and still are) often a playing out of wider geopolitical and religious issues. Shortly before World War One, a theological debate about the relationship between God's Name and God's Essence ended up embroiling the Russian Navy.

8 See, for instance, Peter A. Chambers, trans., 1989, *Nicodemos of the Holy Mountain: A Handbook of Spiritual Counsel*, Classics of Western Spirituality, Mahwah, NJ: Paulist Press.

9 Chambers, *Nicodemos of the Holy Mountain*, p. 161.

10 For instance, see two books by Anglican writers: Simon Barrington-Ward, 2007, *The Jesus Prayer*, Abingdon: BRF, and John Twisleton, 2014, *Using the Jesus Prayer: Steps to a Simpler Christian Life*, Abingdon: BRF. Another indication of this ecumenical reach is the pamphlet on the Jesus Prayer published in 2014 by the Catholic Truth Society but written by Bishop Kallistos Ware.

11 French, trans., *The Way of a Pilgrim*, p. 9.

12 See Rosemary Edmonds, trans., 2020, *St Sophrony, On Prayer: Reflections of a Modern Saint*, New York: SVS Press.

13 From 'The Order for the Administration of the Lord's Supper or Holy Communion' in the Book of Common Prayer.

14 This seems particularly to be part of the Slavic tradition. The following source, for instance, replaces vespers with 600 recitations of the Jesus Prayer and matins with 1,500 recitations: Vladimir Basenkov, 2019, 'Edinovertsi's Treasure: The Rule of Home Prayer', *Orthodox Christianity*, https://orthochristian.com/122042.html, accessed 08.10.2024.

15 Names and place names are given here as they appear in the English translation of the *Philokalia*.

16 Palmer, Ware and Sherrard, trans., *The Philokalia*, vol. 4, pp. 275–86.

17 Palmer, Ware and Sherrard, trans., *The Philokalia*, vol. 4, pp. 69–75.

18 Palmer, Ware and Sherrard, trans., *The Philokalia*, vol. 4, p. 72.

19 Palmer, Ware and Sherrard, trans., *The Philokalia*, vol. 1, p. 262.

20 Palmer, Ware and Sherrard, trans., *The Philokalia*, vol. 4, p. 36. The title is a reference to the 153 fish the disciples catch after the Resurrection in John 21.11.

21 Palmer, Ware and Sherrard, trans., *The Philokalia*, vol. 2, pp. 52–113.

22 Palmer, Ware and Sherrard, trans., *The Philokalia*, vol. 2, p. 55.

23 Palmer, Ware and Sherrard, trans., *The Philokalia*, vol. 2, p. 307.

24 See, for instance, the text attributed to Symeon the New Theologian on prayer quoted above: 'search inside yourself with your intellect so as to find the place of the heart'. Palmer, Ware and Sherrard, trans., *The Philokalia*, vol. 4, p. 72.

25 Palmer, Ware and Sherrard, trans., *The Philokalia*, vol. 4, pp. 205–6.

26 Rowan Williams, 2021, *Looking East in Winter: Contemporary Thought and the Eastern Christian Tradition*, London: Bloomsbury Continuum, p. 29.

27 For the Classical context, see Michel Foucault, 1986, *The Care of the Self: Volume 3 of the History of Sexuality*, New York: Pantheon Books.

28 For a comprehensive review of the relationship between the senses and the soul in Classical and early Christian writings, see Clare Gardom's forthcoming DPhil thesis at the University of Oxford (2026). There is an excellent book on smell in early Christianity: Susan Ashbrook Harvey, 2006, *Scenting Salvation: Ancient Christianity and the Olfactory Imagination*, Oakland, CA: University of California Press.

29 Much Western writing and art on the 'Seven Deadly Sins' can seem somewhat self-indulgent (we need look no further than Dante), but this is not exclusively a Western phenomenon. In the recently restored frescoes at the Church of St Nicholas at Cernica monastery outside Bucharest, various categories of sinners are shown in the lake of fire, among them 'smokers'.

30 Palmer, Ware and Sherrard, trans., *The Philokalia*, vol. 2, pp. 337–40.

31 Palmer, Ware and Sherrard, trans., *The Philokalia*, vol. 1, p. 26.

32 Palmer, Ware and Sherrard, trans., *The Philokalia*, vol. 1, p. 31.

33 Rowan Williams, 2024, *Passions of the Soul*, London: Bloomsbury Continuum, p. 17.

34 Palmer, Ware and Sherrard, trans., *The Philokalia*, vol. 3, p. 23. For more on this story, which is likely autobiographical, see the section on Symeon the New Theologian in Chapter 5, on Divine Light.

35 The most famous of these elders is probably St Seraphim of Sarov.

36 Palmer, Ware and Sherrard, trans., *The Philokalia*, vol. 3, p. 38.

37 Palmer, Ware and Sherrard, trans., *The Philokalia*, vol. 3, p. 177.

38 Palmer, Ware and Sherrard, trans., *The Philokalia*, vol. 3, p. 160.

39 Palmer, Ware and Sherrard, trans., *The Philokalia*, vol. 3, p. 160.

3

The Divine Liturgy: Seeing Heaven

The first time that I attended the Divine Liturgy (what we might call the Eucharist, the Mass or Holy Communion), I had no real idea about what was going on at all. I wasn't even sure when it actually started! The church was quite empty, with a few people bustling around, prayers being said. It was all completely new to me. I had arrived at the advertised start time, but there were no service booklets, or hymn books, or welcomers on the door – none of the Sunday morning apparatus that I was used to. Over the years, I have had various experiences of Orthodox worship in different churches and contexts. The significant diaspora communities in the UK mean it is often not too difficult to find an Orthodox church. When I lived in Oxford, I had the Greek, Russian and Romanian parishes almost on my doorstep! In Romania, I try to go to the Liturgy as often as I can. I can't escape from my own parish and pop to the local cathedral for choral evensong, so the Orthodox Divine Liturgy is where I find spiritual nourishment and refreshment. I always find the expression of piety from the congregation, expressions of sincere faith and love, very moving: lighting candles, venerating the icons, touching written prayers or even photographs of loved ones to the Cross or to the icon of the Mother of God. I feel very comfortable in an Orthodox church. But I am aware that for many Anglicans, Roman Catholics and Protestants, Orthodox worship is completely mystifying: all our norms about when to sit and stand, about participation – joining in the worship – about service sheets and hymn books simply don't apply. As I know from my own first experiences, we simply don't know what to do; whether to copy what everyone else is doing or not; where to stand or how to stand; we don't know where we are in the service, as the Liturgy feels quite different from what we are used to; and so it can be quite overwhelming. On the one hand, we might recognize the aesthetic beauty of a church. We are drawn to the exoticism of the chant and the glimmer of icons in the candlelight. But on the other hand, it can be hard for Western Christians to go beyond those external things into the heart of Orthodox worship. The same exoticism that appeals to us makes it hard to engage with it; we don't know the shape of the Liturgy, the language will likely be one that we don't understand, and often we won't be able to see what is going on in the sanctuary.

Once we have overcome our initial discomfort, however, we find that the differences are not as great as they seem at first. The structure of the Liturgy is not dissimilar to the Western rites, and many Orthodox jurisdictions publish bilingual texts of the prayers for visitors or in the diaspora communities. If we take the time to get to know the Orthodox Liturgy, we can dispel some of the myths ('It's really long!', 'You can come and go as you please!'). As we experience the Liturgy, learn our way around it and come to recognize the prayers, we can find in it true beauty; not the aesthetic beauty of the church and its objects, but the beauty of humanity's offering of praise and thanksgiving to God. The real beauty of the Liturgy is in the worship that we offer, standing side by side, gathered together, with our brothers and sisters in Christ.

In the Orthodox Divine Liturgy, we see a glimpse of heaven – not in the icons and incense and chant, but in the vision of human beings united to each other in love and in the worship of God. The prayer that we offer together in church has all sorts of implications for our mission, our social action and our life together. For in the Liturgy, we see what we are called to be: a community – a church, an assembly – renewed by Christ's Resurrection life. It is in this way that the Liturgy shows us a glimpse of heaven in the earthly sanctuary.

Time and eternity

I mentioned that the first time I attended the Divine Liturgy in an Orthodox church, I wasn't even sure when it began. Often the service of matins, morning prayer, precedes the celebration of the Liturgy itself, and even if this is not the case, before every Liturgy is celebrated, there is a short service of preparation known as the *proskomedia*. From the Greek word for 'offering', this service includes the priest's vesting and the preparation of the bread and the wine that will be used during the Eucharist. It can be surprising to turn up at the advertised time and find things seemingly in full swing! The Divine Liturgy, however, begins with the proclamation, 'Blessed is the kingdom of the Father, and of the Son, and of the Holy Spirit, now and forever and throughout all ages. Amen.'[1]

The first words of the Liturgy are a proclamation of the Kingdom of God. And the Kingdom is at the heart of the vision of the renewed Christian community that the Liturgy gives us, and in which we participate. We see this throughout. Before the Epistle and the Gospel are read, the great manifesto of Kingdom values – the Beatitudes – is usually chanted. We are reminded that the poor in spirit, the meek, the merciful, peacemakers, the persecuted, are all blessed in the Kingdom, contrary to our expectations of worldly success and power. And in the Liturgy, these blessings are framed explicitly to draw us – the congregation – into this vision of a renewed society, where justice and mercy reign: the chanting of the Beatitudes begins with the scriptural prayer, 'O Lord, remember *us* when you come into your kingdom.'[2] The Beatitudes, in this context, present us with a model for our own lives; we are to be the people who inherit, with Christ, the Kingdom of heaven.

And this transformation, this 'becoming', is also seen in the litanies that take place during the Divine Liturgy. The deacon, or priest if there is no deacon, chants a series of petitions, to which the choir responds, 'Lord, have mercy.' These petitions are, first, for the inner peace and salvation of the worshippers, but include petitions for peace in the world, for the Church, the state authorities and armed forces, for seasonable weather, for those travelling, for prisoners, for deliverance from danger and for every necessity. The Liturgy opens with the Great Litany, but there are several of these litanies before the Cherubic Hymn, and also before the Offertory Prayer, and before the Lord's Prayer. Through these litanies, we are praying for the transfiguration of our world; not that we might be delivered from it, or somehow taken out of it and lifted into heaven, but for the flooding of the world with divine grace and for its transformation. In the Liturgy, there is a refashioning of the world into the image of the Kingdom, where there is peace, mercy and where all may find protection and salvation.

So, the Divine Liturgy begins with the proclamation of the Kingdom of God, and it draws us into the mystery of that Kingdom which has not yet come, but which breaks through into our present reality. The Liturgy ties together the historical reality of Christ's life, death and Resurrection, our own times some 2,000 years later, and the future glory of the Kingdom at the culmination of all things. Past, present and future become one equal eternity as, through the Liturgy, we enter sacred time in the Kingdom of God. As Fr Alexander Schmemann, one of the most influential liturgical theologians of the last century, wrote,

> From the beginning the destination is announced: the journey is to the Kingdom. This is where we are going – and not symbolically, but really. In the language of the Bible, which is the language of the Church, to bless the Kingdom is not simply to acclaim it. It is to declare it to be the goal, the end of all our desires and interests, of our whole life, the supreme and ultimate value of all that exists. To bless is to accept in love, and to move toward what is loved.[3]

This theme is wonderfully taken up in an extremely accessible introduction to Orthodox theology and Liturgy, *Journey to the Kingdom*, by Fr Vassilios Papavassiliou.[4] Our journey to the

Kingdom begins when we leave home: we give up the comfort of a Sunday morning lie-in and travel to church, and if no one makes that journey, there can be no Liturgy! And so already the choice to attend worship is an act of sacrificial love.

Like the disciples travelling the Emmaus Road, the Divine Liturgy is a journey we make with the Risen Christ as our companion. The Divine Liturgy is always a celebration of the Resurrection, with every Sunday like a little Easter. We see this in every Eucharist at the proclamation of the Word and in the celebration of the Sacrament. At the Little Entrance, the preparation for the readings, as the Gospel Book is carried aloft through the Royal Doors[5] to the altar, the choir chants, 'Come, let us worship and bow down before Christ. Save us, O Son of God, risen from the dead, we who sing to you: Alleluia!'

Fr Schmemann tells us that the Risen Christ is made present to us in the reading of the Scriptures during the Divine Liturgy: 'For the Gospel is not only a "record" of Christ's resurrection; the Word of God is the eternal coming to us of the Risen Lord, the very power and joy of the resurrection.'[6]

The Risen Christ taught his disciples on the Road to Emmaus, 'beginning with Moses and all the prophets, he interpreted to them the things about himself in all the scriptures' (Luke 24.27). And so the joyful emphasis on the Resurrection in the Divine Liturgy shows that Christ comes alongside us, too, and reveals his presence in the Scriptures.

But this manifestation of the Risen Christ finds its fulfilment in the eucharistic offering itself, bread and wine, taken and blessed. 'For it is you that offer and are offered, who receive and are received, O Christ our God.'[7] The Orthodox Church affirms the full and real presence of Christ in the bread and wine of the Eucharist; they are not merely symbols. The prayer before communion is clear:

I believe, Lord, and I acknowledge, that you are the Christ, the Son of the Living God, who came into the world to save sinners, among whom I am the first. And I believe that this is truly your own most precious Body, and that this is indeed your most precious Blood.

In the Divine Liturgy, the Risen Christ is present with his people. The whole Liturgy is a journey whereby our eyes are opened to Christ walking alongside us, making himself known in the Scriptures and in the breaking of bread. We become witnesses to all that the Lord shows us. After the deacon has taken communion, he exclaims,

> Having beheld the resurrection of Christ, let us worship the holy Lord Jesus ... Come, all you faithful, let us venerate Christ's holy resurrection. For behold, through the cross joy has come to all the world. Let us ever bless the Lord, praising His resurrection, for by enduring the cross for us, He has trampled down death by death.

We worship with the whole company of saints, with all creation, as we share in the joy of the Kingdom through Christ's Resurrection from the dead. At the moment of communion, we are united with Christ, with one another, and with all those holy men and women who worship in the glory of heaven. As the portion of bread designated in honour of the Mother of God is put into the chalice, the pascal joy which we share with the saints is again expressed: 'Shine! Shine! O New Jerusalem! The glory of the Lord has shone upon you! Exult now and be glad, O Zion! Be radiant, O pure Theotokos, in the resurrection of your Son.'

In every celebration of the Liturgy, time passes into eternity, and the Kingdom is opened to us through Christ's Resurrection. To use a phrase from the Church of England's Liturgy, 'the universe resounds with Easter joy and with choirs of angels we sing for ever to your praise.'[8] This joy is ours as we hear the Word and receive the Sacrament, exclaiming, like the disciples at the first Easter, 'We have seen the Lord!' (John 20.25). This is where the Liturgy leads us; this is our journey into the Kingdom. The Divine Liturgy teaches us that the Kingdom of God is not a distant reality but made present in our midst, transforming our

world, and bringing all things to their consummation. To quote
Fr Schmemann,

> The Church is the entrance into the risen life of Christ; it is
> communion in life eternal, 'joy and peace in the Holy Spirit'.
> And it is the expectation of the 'day without evening' of the
> Kingdom; *not of any 'other world' but of the fulfilment of all
> things and all life in Christ.*[9]

Liturgical humanism

As we move beyond the strangeness, beauty and exoticism of the
Liturgy, we see more clearly how Christ is made present to us,
and we are given a glimpse of the Kingdom of God. The Kingdom is not seen in the clouds of incense, in the icons or priestly
vestments, though these things may be a pale reflection of the
heavenly Liturgy. Rather, the Kingdom is made visible in the
reading of the Scriptures, in the offering of bread and wine, and
above all in the Eucharistic community, that is, in the gathering
of Christians together in worship. As Christ himself says, 'For
where two or three are gathered in my name, I am there among
them' (Matthew 18.20).

And this points us to a fundamental truth about our human
nature, about what it means to be human. This is the essential
conviction of Fr Schmemann's liturgical theology, that human
beings are created for worship: the truest expression of our
humanity is in communion with the God who made us and loves
us. He wrote,

> [Worship] is a truly essential act, and man an essentially wor-
> shipping being, for it is only in worship that man has the source
> and the possibility of that knowledge which is communion,
> and of that communion which fulfils itself as true knowledge:
> knowledge of God and therefore knowledge of the world –
> communion with all that exists.[10]

There is a great emphasis in contemporary Orthodox theology on the way that the Liturgy is the place where we are most fully ourselves and where we see true reality. Rowan Williams describes this as a 'liturgical humanism' because it is about the fundamental realities of what it is to be a human person, our liberty (that is, our freedom in Christ), and communion (with God and one another).[11] By contrast, Schmemann argues, secularism is the opposite of this. Secularism is not a 'heresy' about God, but rather, about human beings. He sees the secularizing impulse in our society as a *negation* of the idea of the human person as fundamentally a worshipping being, *homo adorans*.[12] From this perspective, the celebration of the Liturgy is much more than its individual parts, its ritual and ceremonial. Rather, the celebration of the Liturgy is a manifestation of the life of the Kingdom of God, which is both present and future.

Rowan Williams tells us that the question we ask ourselves about the Liturgy in our churches 'is not whether it is instructive, even instantly intelligible, let alone entertaining, but whether it is grounded in listening to the Word and event that has interrupted human [self-centredness]' adding that 'the deepest problem with liturgical practice is a failure to make resurrection visible.'[13] The Liturgy embodies, in the midst of the gathered community, the world-changing power of the Resurrection. Fr Cristian Sonea puts this beautifully:

[The] Resurrection and Ascension transfigured the entire human existence and the world itself. In this sense, Liturgy is meant to show the world in its natural state. It removes the veil placed upon creation so that we can see it as it truly is.[14]

The Liturgy gives us a vision of what we are called to be, standing alongside our brothers and sisters, in the worship of God. In the Liturgy, we see true reality and are given a foretaste of the abundant, eternal life that Jesus promises us.

The implications of this liturgical vision

This vision of the Liturgy helps us to see our worship as a manifestation of the life of the Kingdom of God in the here and now, and it shows us our place in the Kingdom, as the redeemed children of God. The Liturgy, therefore, is a sign to those both inside and outside the Church of what the renewed Christian community should look like, a community of love transfigured by Christ's Resurrection life. This has implications not only for our liturgical practice (both as clergy and laity) but also for the Church's place in our communities and societies.

As in other denominations, there is an awareness in Orthodox understandings of 'mission' that the mission of the Church is nothing other than our human participation in the work of God in the world. 'Mission' is not something that Christians *do* to non-Christians, but a movement of the Spirit in which Christian women and men have a part. That said, Orthodox missiology is more confident about the role of the Church in mission than some of its Western counterparts. For example, the Romanian missiologist Valer Bel describes the role of the Church triumphant, that is, the Church in glory, in the work of God:

> The contribution by the Church triumphant lies in the prayers for the others and the recollection of its members. The biography of the saints did not only play a crucial role in the spiritual guidance of the faithful, it has also made up the most important body of missionary literature in the Orthodox Church. The Church as a whole ... has the duty to carry out the mission.[15]

The mission of the Church, which is nothing other than the work of God in the world, draws together the entire Christian community, lay and ordained, living and departed. This is clearly a vision of mission that is shaped by an understanding of the Divine Liturgy as a manifestation of the Kingdom of God. As we stand side by side with one another in our prayer, surrounded by the saints and angels (literally in the iconography of the Church and mystically in our worship), the living reality of the Kingdom of God breaks through into our lives and our world.

A further (and clear) expression of this liturgical vision is that Orthodox missiologists describe the work of God in the world, in which the Church participates, as 'Liturgy after the Liturgy'. Through the work of Archbishop Anastasios of Albania with the World Council of Churches, beginning in the early 1970s, this phrase has been an important Orthodox contribution to ecumenical discussions on mission. Archbishop Anastasios described the connection between liturgical spirituality and Christian witness:

> The liturgy has to be continued in personal, everyday situations. Each of the faithful is called upon to continue a personal 'liturgy' on the secret altar of his own heart, to realize a living proclamation of the good news 'for the sake of the whole world'. Without this continuation the liturgy remains incomplete.[16]

The idea of extending the celebration of the Liturgy into the ordinary day-to-day of our interactions and experiences is taken up by Cristian Sonea:

> Liturgy is the setting in which all the different expressions of … human existence are brought and offered to God as gifts. As such, all the separate personal forms of existence are proofs of the unity in the Holy Trinity. Accordingly, 'Liturgy after the Liturgy' is an extension of the integrative and unifying experience of the Eucharistic Liturgy into everyday human life.[17]

In the context of parish life, this can take many forms. In my experience of church life in Romania, many Orthodox parishes are involved in social and educational projects, from the informal collection and distribution of food and clothes to those in need, to running residential centres for the elderly.

This invariably touches on what we might call the 'social teaching' of the Orthodox Church. Again, it is clear that this stems from the radical vision of the Liturgy as a manifestation of the Kingdom in our present moment. Drawing on a well-known quotation from the writings of the fourth-century bishop St John Chrysostom, Orthodox social teaching is sometimes referred to as the 'liturgy of the brother'. It comes from a homily on Matthew 25.40: 'Truly I tell you, just as you did it to one of the least of these brothers and sisters of mine, you did it to me.' St John writes,

> Do you want to honour Christ's body? Then do not scorn him in his nakedness, nor honour him here in the church with silken garments while neglecting him outside where he is cold and naked ... For God does not want golden vessels but golden hearts ... Of what use is it to weigh down Christ's table with golden cups, when he himself is dying of hunger? First, fill him when he is hungry; then use the means you have left to adorn his table. Will you have a golden cup made but not give a cup of water? What is the use of providing the table with cloths woven of gold thread, and not providing Christ himself with the clothes he needs? What profit is there in that? ... Do not, therefore, adorn the church and ignore your afflicted brother, for he is the most precious temple of all.[18]

This theme is echoed in the life and writings of the twentieth-century saint, Maria Skobtsova (often known as Mother Maria of Paris). She was born into an aristocratic Russian family, but held socialist views rooted in her religious conviction, and was caught up in the struggle for power in the aftermath of the Bolshevik Revolution. Her young family had moved to Paris by 1923 and following the breakdown of her marriage, she became a nun. She rented a house in Paris, which became a place of refuge for those in need. Mother Maria sheltered Jews at the house following the fall of France in 1940, for which she was sent to Ravensbrück concentration camp and killed in the gas chamber on Holy Saturday 1945. Her whole life was an extension of the liturgical celebration of the Church in the service of the poor and needy. She wrote,

So many talk about the necessity of giving our entire existence an ecclesiastic dimension, but very few understand what that means. Does it mean attending every church service? Or does it mean putting an icon in every room and lighting a candle? No. Giving an ecclesiastic dimension to our lives means seeing the entire world as a church full of icons that deserve to be venerated, honoured and loved for being the authentic faces of God in which the holiness of the Living God rests.[19]

As we see in the writings of St John Chrysostom and Mother Maria of Paris, to live 'liturgically', and to be rooted in the liturgical worship of the Church, is not a kind of escapism. We can be distracted by the externals of worship or the particular details of our ceremonial, but as noted in the words of Rowan Williams earlier, 'the deepest problem with liturgical practice is a failure to make resurrection visible.'[20] Our Liturgy must embody the power of Christ's Resurrection to change our lives and our world. In such a vision of the liturgical life of the Church, our worship extends far beyond the walls of the church building into those places and parts of our lives that so badly need Christ's light. The Liturgy is lived out and the good news of the Kingdom of God is proclaimed. As the Divine Liturgy begins, 'Blessed is the kingdom of the Father, and of the Son, and of the Holy Spirit, now and forever and throughout all ages', so that proclamation continues to resound in our hearts as we go about our daily lives, among our families and friends, at work and at home. Through the beauty we experience in worship, the Liturgy points us to the worship of heaven, but it also does so much more. Through Christ's Resurrection, the Liturgy draws us into the present reality of the Kingdom of God, breaking through all the hard-heartedness and sin of our world, and invites us to live the life of heaven in the here and now.

Notes

1 Quotations from the Liturgy are taken, unless otherwise indicated, from the bilingual Romanian-English, David Frost, trans., 2015, *Divine Liturgy of St John Chrysostom*, Cambridge: IOCS. The Liturgy of St John Chrysostom is the most commonly celebrated Liturgy in the Byzantine tradition. The Liturgy of St Basil the Great is used ten times a year, including the Sundays of Lent, Maundy Thursday, Holy Saturday and Christmas Eve. On weekdays in Lent, the Liturgy of the Presanctified Gifts, attributed to Gregory the Great, is used. The Liturgy of St James, reflecting the ancient tradition of the Church in Jerusalem, is occasionally celebrated, and even more rarely the Alexandrian Liturgy of St Mark.

2 The third antiphon in the Liturgy of St John Chrysostom. My emphasis.

3 Alexander Schmemann, 1998, *For the Life of the World: Sacraments and Orthodoxy*, New York: SVS Press, p. 29.

4 Vassilios Papavassiliou, 2012, *Journey to the Kingdom: An Insider's Look at the Liturgy and Beliefs of the Eastern Orthodox Church*, Brewster, MA: Paraclete Press.

5 The Royal Doors are the central doors of the icon screen, separating the sanctuary from the main body of the church.

6 Schmemann, *For the Life of the World: Sacraments and Orthodoxy*, p. 33.

7 The priest's prayer during the Cherubic Hymn.

8 *Common Worship*, Extended Preface for Ascension Day.

9 Schmemann, *For the Life of the World: Sacraments and Orthodoxy*, p. 106. My emphasis.

10 Schmemann, *For the Life of the World: Sacraments and Orthodoxy*, p. 120.

11 Rowan Williams, 2021, *Looking East in Winter: Contemporary Thought and the Eastern Christian Tradition*, London: Bloomsbury Continuum, pp. 156–7.

12 See Chad Hatfield, 2022, 'The Eucharist as Antidote to Secularism: Insights from a Twentieth-Century American Orthodox Perspective' in Daniel Munteanu and Sorin Şelaru, eds, *Holding Fast to the Mystery of Faith: Festschrift for Patriarch Daniel of the Romanian Orthodox Church*, Leiden: Brill, pp. 224–5.

13 Williams, *Looking East in Winter*, p. 157.

14 Cristian Sonea, 2020, 'The "Liturgy after the Liturgy" and Deep Solidarity: The Orthodox Understanding of Christian Witness and its Implications for Human Society', *Mission Studies*, 37, p. 454.

15 Valer Bel and Radu Preda, 2013, 'The Development of Missionary

and Social Studies' in Viorel Ioniţă, ed., *Orthodox Theology in the 20th Century and Early 21st Century: A Romanian Orthodox Perspective*, Bucharest: Basilica, p. 713.

16 Cited in Ion Bria, 1978, 'The Liturgy after the Liturgy', *International Review of Mission*, 67, p. 86.

17 Sonea, 'The "Liturgy after the Liturgy" and Deep Solidarity', p. 454.

18 Text taken from the *Divine Office*, Office of Readings for the 21st Week in Ordinary Time.

19 Cited in Sonea, 'The "Liturgy after the Liturgy" and Deep Solidarity', p. 457. For a profound and accessible collection of Mother Maria's writings, see Richard Pevear and Larissa Volokhonsky, trans., 2003, *Mother Maria Skobtsova: Essential Writings*, Modern Spiritual Masters Series, Maryknoll, NY: Orbis Books.

20 Williams, *Looking East in Winter*, p. 157.

4

Byzantine Hymnody:
Seeing the Scriptures

When I was a student, St Catharine's College in Cambridge had an evening service, sung by the Girls' Choir, called Luminaria. It was a specially devised, atmospheric evening service, a celebration of Christ the Light of the World. After the opening prayer, the choir would sing a hymn in Greek, the *Phos Hilaron*, 'O joyful light'. When I first heard it, the hymn had an almost ethereal quality, as a solo voice began to sing the first line of this haunting melody in an unfamiliar language. It somehow even sounded ancient.

The *Phos Hilaron* was probably composed in the third century, possibly earlier, and is the oldest known Christian hymn outside the Bible. Even in the fourth century, the *Phos Hilaron* was considered old: Basil of Caesarea described the hymn as an ancient formula and its recitation as a pious act. It was written to be sung at the lighting of the lamps in the evening, contrasting Christ, the luminous glory of the Father, with the fading light of the setting sun. The *Phos Hilaron* is still used daily at vespers in the Orthodox churches, and it is familiar as an evening hymn in the English-speaking world through John Keble's translation, 'Hail, gladdening Light'. This remarkable hymn connects our worship across time and space, across denominations and languages.

Despite this continuity between East and West, however, Orthodox chant can seem as mystifying and exotic as icons or the experience of the Divine Liturgy. It is one of the things that visitors to an Orthodox church will be struck by and instinctively feel as different from the Western traditions of church music. There are a couple of reasons for this. First, the interaction between the choir, the priest and the congregation is not the same as in modern Western liturgies. While it varies from place to place and the type of service, most of the hymnody will be sung by the choir, and the congregation will join in only for the most well-known hymns. This is, in part, because there is so much variable liturgical material. I have an entire shelf of Orthodox liturgical books, and it is by no means a comprehensive collection! The singing of the choir is also used to cover other parts of the liturgical action that often happen out of sight of the congregation. Historically, this also happened in the West, but in modern times it can feel like an unfamiliar approach to our participation in worship.

Second, and perhaps more significantly, Orthodox chant seems so exotic to Western ears because it uses an entirely different musical system. Each note on a musical scale corresponds to a specific pitch. When we play a scale, say on a piano, we play a consecutive series of notes by order of pitch. One of the key differences between Byzantine chant and Western musical traditions is that Byzantine chant contains intervals between pitches that simply don't exist in Western music. We could approximate them on a piano, but it would not be quite accurate. In the West, a 'mode' refers to the fixed notes on a scale, whereas in Byzantine chant, the eight modes reflect the grouping of relative pitches. This gives the chanter a great deal more freedom and flexibility in singing. Byzantine chant also developed a whole system of notation independently of Western stave notation. It looks very beautiful on the page, but it is incomprehensible until you've learnt the principles! Another distinctive feature that is immediately noticeable is the bass drone, the 'ison' that accompanies the melody in Byzantine chant, which lends it a distinctive sound. The hymns and chant of the Orthodox Church reflect a distinct tradition that differs from the development of church music in the West, which is why it sounds so unusual to Western Christians.

Orthodox hymns are written in a variety of styles, of varying lengths, and for use at different services or parts of the Liturgy.

By way of introduction, there are four kinds of hymns that we will consider. First, there is the *troparion*. This is a short, one-stanza hymn that reflects the liturgical feast or the theme of the day. In this way, its function is a bit like the collect in Anglican and Catholic Liturgy. The *kontakion* is a long metrical hymn with a short refrain. It was originally a homily in verse, and probably designed so that the congregation could join in with the refrain. The *kontakion* was gradually replaced in popularity by the *canon*, another long, structured hymn that incorporates biblical material and links it with the themes particular to the day. *Stichera* are short hymns that are sung between verses of psalmody or other biblical texts. We will come back to these four kinds of hymn.

The study of Orthodox hymnody is a complex and technical business, reflecting the interaction of musical theory, poetics and patristics. As in Western traditions, hymns are a rich source of theology and devotion. In a quotation attributed to St Gregory Palamas, we read: 'Whoever attunes himself and studies the meaning of sacred songs from the beginning to end, will find himself approaching God.' Orthodox hymnody is also deeply rooted in Scripture and can teach us how to engage more profoundly with the Bible.

I once went to the launch of a new bilingual Romanian-Greek New Testament, based on a Byzantine Greek manuscript from Vatopedi monastery on Mount Athos. I had seen the event advertised through the Theology Faculty, so I had a clear idea in my mind about what the book launch would be like: a small room, maybe a glass of wine and some speeches about the technical aspects of biblical translation. I was completely astonished to discover it was in the great hall of the Palace of the Patriarchate, which was overflowing with people. There were students and priests, but also families with their children. The event was presided over by the Patriarch and the guest of honour was Elder Ephraim of Vatopedi, who is a popular spiritual figure. Afterwards, copies of this New Testament (which was beautifully illustrated and produced) were being given away, and the thronging of the crowd was extraordinary! I have never known anything like it. I am certain that the vast majority of the people there could not read Byzantine Greek, but their enthusiasm for the biblical text was remarkable.

I have met Christians from Reformed traditions who assume Orthodox Christians sit lightly to the Bible, but that is certainly not the case. In my experience, general biblical literacy in Romania is significantly higher than in the UK. People still know the stories. One of the reasons for this is that many Old Testament prophets are venerated in the liturgical calendar of the Church, with their own feast days and icons. The commemoration of the Prophet Elijah on 20 July, for instance, is an important festival in Romania. Were you to ask people on the streets of the UK about Elijah, you'd probably be met with a blank look.

Another reason that so many Romanians that I have met still know the biblical stories is because a lot of Scripture is read or chanted in Orthodox worship! And in a profound way, the great hymn writers of the Orthodox Church used their hymns as a way of drawing people into the stories of the Bible. The Byzantine scholar Andrew Mellas puts this beautifully:

> Hymnographers invited the congregations of Constantinople to enter the story song of their hymns, asking them to become part of the divine economy of salvation and to feel the emotions of biblical characters. The scriptural narrative of this divine economy and the actions of God's people came together in a liturgical panorama. Hymnody envisioned a communion of saints and embodied a mystical harmony between humanity and creation ... Hymnody embodied and enacted a mystical vision where liturgical emotions could be perceived and felt in the singer's encounter with the Divine.[1]

We will explore how Orthodox hymns allow the language of Scripture to shape our imaginations. This can give us a fresh perspective on familiar texts, drawing *us* in, and thus helping to make the biblical story *our* story.

Romanos the Melodist, Syriac poetry and Scripture

One of my recurring dreams is that I am leading worship but as soon as I look at the page of the Gospel book or the missal, the words just don't make any sense. I simply cannot read what is written and stumble through them. While this has never happened to me in real life, I would be in good company. At the Christmas Eve vigil in 518, a young man called Romanos stood up to chant from the Psalter in the Church of the Panagia in Constantinople. He tripped over the words and read so badly that someone else had to take over from him. He was mocked by the other members of the choir, and sank back into one of the choir stalls, no doubt wishing a hole would swallow him up. Worn out by the whole experience, he fell asleep. As he slept, the Mother of God appeared to him and told him to eat the scroll she was holding in her hand. He awoke, and then getting up from his seat, he made his way to the reading desk in the middle of the church. He then sang beautifully, chanting extemporaneously the *kontakion* that is now sung every Christmas, 'Today the Virgin gives birth to the One above all being.' The entire congregation, Emperor and Patriarch among them, were astonished by this young man's voice and his ability to articulate theology in verse so profoundly.

Little is known about Romanos' life. He was born in Emesa (modern-day Homs), Syria, in the late fifth century to a Jewish family. Following his conversion to Christianity as a boy, he moved to Beirut where he was ordained deacon, and then to Constantinople where he remained until his death. His poetry is full of scriptural allusions, connecting the stories of the Old Testament with the life of Jesus, weaving layers of meaning together.[2] Romanos gives expression to the thoughts and feelings of the characters of the biblical stories. For instance, in his poem on the Rich Man and Lazarus from Luke 16, Romanos imagines the circumstances of Lazarus' life, his dependence on God and his trust in God's mercy, making explicit what is implicit in the text. This creative and poetic approach to Scripture draws on our emotions, makes the stories of the Bible come alive for us, and helps us to see them in new ways.

The legend about Romanos' miraculous singing in the Church of the Panagia attributes the genre of hymns known as *kontakia* to him. It is certainly the case that Romanos popularized and developed the genre in Greek-speaking Constantinople, but these verse homilies with a simple refrain originated in the Syriac-speaking world where Romanos grew up. The distinctive way that Byzantine hymnody engages, explores and imagines Scripture springs from the poetic traditions of the Christian Near East.

Syriac emerged as a literary language among Christian communities in the region encompassing modern Turkey, Syria, Iraq and Iran. Linguistically, it is related to the Aramaic which had once been the *lingua franca* of the Ancient Near East and to the language that Jesus would have spoken. The Syriac-speaking churches have a complex history and over the course of the first centuries of Christianity, they divided for a range of theological, political and geographical reasons. These churches reflect a profound theological legacy that is often overlooked in the history of Christianity, and they have often suffered persecution in their homelands. They preserve a rich heritage that can offer us new perspectives and ways of understanding, which is a great gift to the universal Church. The poetry and hymns of St Ephrem the Syrian are probably the most well-known examples of this heritage, but there are many other writers who follow in St Ephrem's footsteps and give us striking poetic insights into the stories of Scripture.

Owing to its long literary history, the genres of Syriac poetry stretch right back into the world of Ancient Mesopotamia. For one fascinating genre, the dialogue poem, we have examples in Sumerian that are at least 4,000 years old. These poems take the form of precedence disputes: two or more figures argue about who is better, or who is in the right. The genre takes on a new life in the hands of Christian authors exploring the biblical text. Dialogue poems take a particular moment in a biblical story, usually a moment of tension, and the voices argue in alternating verses. This requires a rich imagination as the scene is set and the dialogue unfolds. Sometimes they are quite funny, as with the poem on Joseph's encounter with Potiphar's wife in Genesis 39.[3] At other times, they are quite profound: one such poem is an argument between the Cherub guarding the way to Paradise with his flaming sword (as in Genesis 3.24) and the Penitent Thief crucified with Christ.[4] The Cherub tells the Thief he cannot enter Paradise, but he is eventually won over when the Thief tells him about the Crucifixion.

These poems often give voice to the voiceless characters of Scripture. There is a poetic dialogue, for instance, between the anonymous woman in Luke 7.36–50 and Satan.[5] In the scriptural account the woman is silent, she doesn't speak at all, but in the poem, she extols the loving mercy of God and the virtue of repentance. In one notable example, even the River Jordan is given a voice in a poem that establishes the Jordan's precedence over the other rivers of the Bible on account of Christ's baptism.[6]

Alongside St Ephrem the Syrian, another of the great Syriac poet-theologians is Jacob of Serugh. He died in the year 521, and so he was a slightly older contemporary of Romanos the Melodist. Jacob was a very prolific writer who composed some 380 poetic homilies, written in a distinctive 12-syllable metre that is named after him. While some of these poems are written for the feasts of the liturgical year, they are usually based on a biblical story. In one poem, on Tamar and Judah (based on Genesis 38), we are shown clearly how Jacob understands Scripture:

> Moses the scribe set the story of Tamar
> like a jewel in his Book so that its beauty might shine out
> amongst its lections.
> Why would he have written of a woman who sat like a
> prostitute
> by the crossroads had she not been filled with some mystery?[7]

The biblical text always contains some spiritual truth, and Jacob's poetic explorations of the stories help us to uncover their treasure. In the poem on Tamar and Judah, Tamar's faith becomes an example to follow:

> O soul who, like a prostitute, loves the world
> supplicate Christ by the wayside, and once you have found
>   him,
> take refuge in faith that is filled with light.[8]

The Syriac poetic tradition presents us with a way of engaging with the Scriptures imaginatively and creatively. Through the imagined dialogue and the articulation of the characters' inner thoughts, we can read the stories of the Bible in new and exciting ways.

Importantly, it is this tradition of exegesis that Romanos brings to the Greek-speaking world of Constantinople through his hymns. While he wrote in Greek, he was certainly bilingual. Sometimes his poetry requires biblical names to be scanned as they would be in Syriac, or he quotes from Bible texts as they appear in Syriac sources. He shares images and metaphors with the poetry of St Ephrem, and the *kontakion* clearly derives from the genre of verse homilies with a refrain that is found in Syriac. Romanos may not have invented the *kontakion* as a poetic form, but through him, this tradition of exploring the Scriptures through poetry, of giving voice to the characters of the Bible, finds a wide audience and becomes a treasure of Orthodox hymnody.

Kassiani: a woman's voice in Byzantine hymnody

If the *kontakia* genre gives a voice to the voiceless characters of the scriptural story, as we have seen in Romanos the Melodist and the Syriac tradition, then this aspect of Byzantine hymnody takes on a new significance in the works of St Kassiani. Writing in the ninth century, Kassiani (sometimes called Kassia) is the first known female composer whose music can be interpreted by modern scholars and musicians.[9] She is the only named woman whose works appear in the liturgical books of the Orthodox Church, with roughly 50 hymns attributed to her in medieval manuscripts (though only a handful of these hymns are still in use today).[10] While the texts of Byzantine hymns express the inner thoughts and feelings of those in Scripture who do not otherwise speak, in Kassiani we find the singular expression of a woman's voice in the hymns of the Orthodox Church.

Kassiani was born in the early years of the ninth century, at Constantinople. As a young woman in the 820s, she was in contact with St Theodore the Studite and three of his letters to her survive. They indicate that her father probably held office in an elite group of imperial guards, the *kandidatoi*. But the letters also testify to Kassiani's education, her defence of the veneration of icons (opposing the imperial policy of iconoclasm at that time) and her desire to pursue her vocation in a religious community. Her early communication with St Theodore no doubt helped shape her interest in the Liturgy and her skill as a hymnographer; Theodore was himself an accomplished poet, and the Stoudios monastery that he revived became an important centre of liturgical reform in Constantinople. The role of the monastery in the production of liturgical books over the ninth and tenth centuries also contributed to the survival and circulation of Kassiani's work.

According to legend, Kassiani took part in an imperial 'bride show' when the Emperor Theophilus was searching for a wife. He was struck by her beauty, but as Kassiani responded to him with wit and courage, the Emperor's pride was wounded and he rejected her. Kassiani became a nun, founding her own community following the end of iconoclasm with the Council of Constantinople in 843.

Today, Kassiani is most well-known for a hymn appointed for matins on the Wednesday of Holy Week (which in current practice is sung on the Tuesday evening). It is a beautiful and striking hymn of repentance, and it is theologically profound. As with the

Syriac dialogue poem and Romanos' *kontakion* on this passage, Kassiani's hymn voices the thoughts of the penitent woman who anoints Christ's feet in Luke 7.

> Lord, the woman who had fallen into many sins, perceiving your divinity, took up the role of myrrh-bearer, and with lamentation brings sweet myrrh to you before your burial. 'Alas!' she says, 'for night is for me a frenzy of lust, a dark and moonless love of sin. Accept the fountains of my tears, you who from the clouds draw out the water of the sea; bow yourself down to the groanings of my heart, you who bowed the heavens by your ineffable self-emptying. I shall kiss your immaculate feet, and wipe them again with the locks of my hair, those feet whose sound Eve heard at dusk in Paradise, and hid herself in fear. Who can search out the multitude of my sins and the depths of your judgements, my Saviour, saviour of souls? Do not despise me, your servant, for you have mercy without measure.'[11]

There are a number of threads that we can draw out of this hymn that give us new perspectives on the Gospel passage. First, Kassiani describes the woman as taking up the role of 'myrrh-bearer'. This passage is connected to Christ's coming burial, through the image of lament and anointing. But 'myrrh-bearer' is also the title used in Orthodoxy of the women who went to Christ's tomb on Easter morning, so Kassiani connects this event before Christ's death with his Resurrection, also revealed in the woman's trust in Christ's mercy and as the one who saves. The reference to washing Christ's feet, the same feet whose sound was heard in the Garden of Eden, connects the Old Testament with the New and points to the Orthodox hermeneutic by which the Old Testament appearances of God are always the pre-incarnate Christ. Last, it is a very emotive and expressive hymn that models repentance for those who hear it. As this hymn is sung during Holy Week, we are made aware of our own sin and our complete dependence on God's mercy. This woman's story becomes our story. As Andrew Mellas notes, 'Liturgical hymns were not simply a remembrance of biblical events or a theatrical display of divine things; they enacted a sacred drama that created a space of participation for the faithful in the mystery of salvation.'[12]

These theologically rich strands of Kassiani's Holy Week hymn (often simply referred to as the 'Hymn of Kassiani') can also be seen in her other extant hymns, even though these are less well-known, and show how hymnody can be used as a way of shaping our understanding of the Scriptures.

The typological connection between the Old and New Testaments is often expressed in these hymns. While the story of the crossing of the Red Sea in Exodus, a passing through death, was from earliest days associated with Easter, Kassiani takes the drowning of Pharaoh and connects it to Christ's death in a hymn for Holy Saturday. The one who drowned Pharaoh and his army is buried in the tomb: 'He who once hid the pursuing tyrant in the waves of the sea, was hidden beneath the earth.'[13] Kassiani's understanding of Christ's divinity means that the Old Testament speaks just as clearly about him as the Gospels. Christ is present and active in all the words of sacred Scripture.

The relationship between Kassiani's hymns and the Scriptures goes beyond the images and stories that she uses. The liturgical context of these hymns also has a bearing on how we use them to understand the Bible. As the Hymn of Kassiani on Holy Wednesday stands as a call to repentance for the congregation gathered in worship, these hymns help us to interpret the scriptural passages around them. For instance, Kassiani wrote a series of short hymns (*stichera*) for use on Christmas Eve. These hymns are interspersed between verses from Psalm 130 (Psalm 129 according to the Orthodox Psalter), and thus provide a gloss on their meaning. As one of the standard psalms sung at vespers, Kassiani's short hymns provide a seasonal interpretation of the passages that are used. The verse, 'O let your ears be attentive, to the voice of my supplication' is followed by a meditation on the Incarnation: 'a company of angels from on high praised your great concession towards mankind, Who through the deepest compassion put on a body and deified the garment of mortals, glory to you.'[14]

Taken together, we can understand the Psalmist's appeal to God as answered in Christ's birth, emphasizing God's attentiveness and compassion towards humanity's need. The same refrain is used in the next *sticheron*: 'Lord, who through the deepest compassion put on flesh and deified the garment of mortals, glory to you.' This time the preceding verses are Psalm 130.3–5: 'If you, O Lord, should mark iniquities, Lord, who will stand? But there is forgiveness with you.' By this juxtaposition, Kassiani shows us the depths of God's mercy and highlights the role of the Incarnation in our salvation. Kassiani's hymns provide us with a hermeneutic tool for understanding Scripture in its liturgical context.

Kassiani's famous hymn follows the ancient tradition in Eastern hymnody of giving expression to the inner thoughts and feelings of the women and men of the Bible. As well as the anonymous 'myrrh-bearer', one of the Christmas Eve *stichera* voices Mary's astonishment at the Incarnation:

When you appeared, Christ, made flesh from a woman, she who bore you, astounded by your condescension, tearfully said, 'Saviour, how can I bear you as infant who are eternal? How can I nourish with milk you who nourish the whole of creation with your divine power?'[15]

And like the earlier traditions, Kassiani also gives voice to all created things. In a verse describing the Crucifixion, the whole of creation laments for Christ: 'When the creation observed you hanging on Golgotha, who without hindrance hung the whole earth upon the waters, it was filled with great astonishment and cried out, "There is no one holy except you, O Lord!"'[16] The capacity of these hymns to express the emotions and drama of the events of the Bible extends to all that exists.

Kassiani, the lone female voice of Byzantine hymnody, gives a theologically rich dimension to the liturgical life of the Church and its interpretation of Scripture. Her hymns draw us into the sacred drama and make the stories of Scripture part of our own stories. This is clear in a short hymn for vespers at the start of the Lenten season:

> Almighty Lord, I know how powerful tears are. They brought Ezekias up from the gates of death.[17] They delivered the sinful woman from the transgressions of many years. They justified the Tax Collector above the Pharisee. And so I pray, 'Numbering me with them, have mercy on me.'[18]

In these few lines, framed in the first person, three scriptural models of repentance are presented. At the end, we become woven into the fabric of the Bible's narrative of repentance and mercy, explicitly joining our act of penitence with theirs. This aspect of Kassiani's hymn writing, making the scriptural story our story, leads us to the longest of Orthodox hymns, the Great Canon of St Andrew of Crete.

The Great Canon: entering into the scriptural story

The Great Canon, also known as the Canon of Repentance, was composed by St Andrew of Crete some time in the seventh century. A canon is a structured hymn, split into nine odes, each made up of a number of verses linked by a refrain. The Great Canon has 250 of these verses, making it by far the longest of this type of hymn. It is divided up and sung over four nights at the start of Lent, and again in its entirety at matins on the Thursday of the fifth week of Lent (in current practice on Wednesday evening). It is a meditation on repentance and humility, written in the first person as a dialogue with the soul. The Great Canon works through the scriptural narrative to draw on biblical models of contrition, encouraging the soul to imitate the good deeds of the righteous and to turn away from sin. This intention is made explicit in the Canon itself: 'All the names of the Old Testament have I set before thee, my soul, as an example. Imitate the holy acts of the righteous and flee from the sins of the wicked' (Ode 8, 12).[19] And again,

> I bring thee, O my soul, examples from the New Testament, to lead thee to compunction. Follow the example of the righteous, turn away from the sinful, and through prayers and fasting, through chastity and reverence, win back Christ's mercy. (Ode 9, 4)

A specific example of this can be seen in the Great Canon's reference to the story of Cain and Abel. The first-person narrator, which we are each to understand as ourselves, is likened to the murderer Cain, but the good example of the righteous Abel is held before us:

> By my own free choice have I incurred the guilt of Cain's murder. I have killed my conscience, bringing the flesh to life and making war upon the soul by my wicked actions.
> *Have mercy on me, O God, have mercy on me.*
> O Jesus, I have not been like Abel in his righteousness. Never have I offered Thee acceptable gifts or godly actions, a pure sacrifice or an unblemished life. (Ode 1, 7–8)

The fact that St Andrew of Crete draws on examples from throughout the Bible means that there are often interesting interpretations of biblical stories, ways of making the Bible part of our experience. For instance, in the section on Jacob in Ode IV, there is a reference to Jacob's wives: 'By the two wives, understand action and knowledge in contemplation. Leah is action, for she had many children; and Rachel is knowledge, for she endured great toil. For without toil, O my soul, neither action nor contemplation will succeed' (Ode 4, 8).

As we have seen in the hymns of Romanos and Kassiani, these theological interpretations of the Bible are often innovative and thought-provoking. There is also a significant emphasis on seeing the events of the Old Testament as mirroring aspects of the life of Christ. As Kassiani contrasts the drowning of Pharoah in the Red Sea with Christ's burial, St Andrew of Crete sees the moment when Joseph's brothers throw him into the well as a foreshadowing of Christ's burial and Resurrection: 'Once Joseph was cast into a pit, O Lord and Master, as a figure of Thy Burial and Resurrection' (Ode 5, 6). The verses of the Great Canon are a mine of biblical interpretation and imagery.

The deeply personal tone that St Andrew uses in the Great Canon is not intended as an autobiographical account of his own sinfulness and need of God's mercy, but as a way of making the Canon speak to every human heart. In all the examples that he uses, the specific stories and events of the Bible are used to draw us and our souls into the sacred story, the story of humanity in relation to God. The recitation of this hymn is a rich source of inspiration in the Lenten season. Over the centuries, people have written commentaries on the Great Canon, explaining the references, drawing on other material, expounding the meaning of particular words, and this shows us how Byzantine hymnody can be a living, breathing tradition that is ever relevant to us in our spiritual growth.

Our exploration of Byzantine hymnody, through the writings of Romanos, Kassiani and St Andrew of Crete, shows us what spiritual treasure this tradition contains. Above all, these hymn writers teach us how to make the words and language of Scripture our own. They encourage us to allow Scripture to shape our imaginations, to express ourselves in the language of Scripture, to read and understand the stories of the Bible in new ways, and to make the biblical story the story of our own souls in relationship with the Divine.

Notes

1 Andrew Mellas, 2020, *Liturgy and the Emotions in Byzantium: Compunction and Hymnody*, Cambridge: Cambridge University Press, p. 170.

2 For instance, the miracle of the axe head in 2 Kings 6 is taken as a foreshadowing of salvation through the Cross. Andrew Mellas, trans., 2020, *Hymns of Repentance: Saint Romanos the Melodist*, New York: SVS Press, p. 97.

3 Sebastian Brock, trans., 2012, *Treasure-house of Mysteries: Explorations of the Sacred Text through Poetry in the Syriac Tradition*, New York: SVS Press, pp. 104–7.

4 Brock, *Treasure-house of Mysteries*, pp. 220–9.

5 Brock, *Treasure-house of Mysteries*, pp. 201–10.

6 Brock, *Treasure-house of Mysteries*, pp. 31–5.

7 Brock, *Treasure-house of Mysteries*, p. 92.

8 Brock, *Treasure-house of Mysteries*, pp. 103–4.

9 Under the direction of Alexander Lingas, Cappella Romana produced a CD of Kassiani's music in 2021. Alexander Lingas and Cappella Romana, 2021, *Hymns of Kassiani*, Bristol: Cappella Records.

10 There is one other female composer, who is recorded simply as the daughter of Ioannes Kladas (himself a famous musician in late fourteenth-century Constantinople). She composed a single antiphon that is included in a manuscript collection of her father's works.

11 Liner notes to Lingas and Cappella Romana, *Hymns of Kassiani*, p. 13.

12 Mellas, *Liturgy and the Emotions in Byzantium*, p. 19.

13 Liner notes to Lingas and Cappella Romana, *Hymns of Kassiani*, p. 11.

14 Liner notes to Lingas and Cappella Romana, *Hymns of Kassiani*, p. 9.

15 Liner notes to Lingas and Cappella Romana, *Hymns of Kassiani*, p. 9.

16 Liner notes to Lingas and Cappella Romana, *Hymns of Kassiani*, p. 11.

17 A reference to 2 Kings 20.

18 Liner notes to Lingas and Cappella Romana, *Hymns of Kassiani*, p. 11.

19 The translations of texts from the Great Canon are taken from Mother Mary and Kallistos Ware, trans., 2002 (reprint), *The Lenten Triodion*, Waymart, PA: St Tikhon's Seminary Press, pp. 378–415.

5

Divine Light: Seeing the Holy Spirit

I remember my confirmation for the wrong reason! I was in my mid-teens, confirmed by the Bishop of Hertford in my parish church, along with my sister and several others. I'm not sure what I was expecting, but I do remember being slightly underwhelmed as the bishop laid his hand on my head and prayed, 'Confirm, O Lord, your servant with your Holy Spirit.' Perhaps I wanted the warm, fuzzy glow of the Spirit's presence, or maybe a dramatic and flaming sign of the indwelling of the Spirit. But it was neither. Instead, my abiding memory of my confirmation is receiving as a gift my first mobile phone from my parents, a small and solid Nokia 3310.

Confirmation does not exist as a separate liturgical celebration in the Orthodox Church (except for the reception of converts) and instead takes place in the context of the baptismal Liturgy. This is why babies can also receive Communion in the Orthodox Church. In Orthodoxy, it is usually called chrismation rather than confirmation, referring to the use of holy oil, chrism. The sign of the Cross is made on the candidate's forehead, eyes, nostrils, mouth, ears, chest, hands and feet, and each time, the priest says, 'the seal of the gift of the Holy Spirit'. The separation of confirmation from baptism in the Western Church is a historical curiosity, but it highlights some of the quite distinctive differences between the ways the Holy Spirit is understood in the Eastern and Western churches.

The Holy Spirit: East and West

There are some very beautiful hymns and prayers to the Holy Spirit in the Western tradition. We might think of the ninth-century 'Veni creator spiritus', which was included in the Church of England's ordination services. It was first translated by Cranmer for the ordinal of 1550, his only foray into verse translation. The translation most widely known today, however, was made by Bishop John Cosin for the Coronation of Charles I, and included in the 1662 Book of Common Prayer: 'Come, Holy Ghost, our souls inspire.' One of my favourite hymns is a translation of a prayer of Bianco da Siena (d. 1434):

> Come down, O Love divine,
> seek thou this soul of mine,
> and visit it with thine own ardour glowing;
> O Comforter, draw near,
> within my heart appear,
> and kindle it, thy holy flame bestowing.

But as well as these translations of medieval hymns to the Spirit, there is a rich vein of devotion to the Holy Spirit in Anglican spirituality. We might think of George Herbert's poem, 'Whitsunday', which begins:

> Listen sweet Dove unto my song,
> And spread thy golden wings in me;
> Hatching my tender heart so long,
> Till it get wing, and flie away with thee.

Following his evangelical conversion in 1738, John Wesley came to place a great emphasis on the role of the Holy Spirit in the sanctification of the Christian person. In a letter that he wrote to a Roman Catholic, Wesley outlined this belief:

> I believe the infinite and eternal Spirit of God, equal with the Father and the Son, to be not only perfectly holy in himself,

but the immediate cause of all holiness in us: enlightening our understandings, rectifying our wills and affections, renewing our natures, uniting our persons to Christ, assuring us of the adoption of sons, leading us in our actions, purifying and sanctifying our souls and bodies, to a full and eternal enjoyment of God.[1]

John and Charles Wesley also wrote an entire collection of hymns for Pentecost, published in 1746 with the title *Hymns of Petition and Thanksgiving for the Promise of the Father.*

But despite this rich inheritance, our contemporary liturgical material too often relegates the Spirit to the feast of Pentecost and to the Trinitarian doxology that concludes our prayers. We are not very good at talking about the Holy Spirit. By contrast, public and private prayer in the Orthodox tradition always begins with an invocation of the Spirit. 'Heavenly King, Comforter, Spirit of Truth; you are everywhere present and fill all things. Treasury of blessings and Giver of Life, come and dwell within us; cleanse us of all stain; and save our souls, O Gracious One.'

Whether it's in the morning or evening, at home or in church, or in the celebration of the Divine Liturgy, this prayer is almost always used, preparing the hearts of the faithful for worship. It is a beautiful prayer that says profound things about the way the Spirit is at work in our lives. The prayer was translated and put into verse by the Glaswegian Free Church minister John Brownlie (d. 1925) and appears in several Anglican hymnals.[2]

> O King enthroned on high,
> thou Comforter divine,
> blest Spirit of all truth, be nigh
> and make us thine.
>
> Thou art the source of life;
> thou art our treasure-store;
> give us thy peace, and end our strife
> for evermore.

> Descend, O heavenly Dove,
> abide with us always;
> and in the fulness of thy love
> cleanse us, we pray.

The simple fact that Orthodox worship always begins with this prayer to the Holy Spirit reflects the 'Charismatic' and 'Pentecostal' character of the Orthodox Church! The Holy Spirit is not an 'add-on' to Christian belief about the nature of God. This is something that is brought out very powerfully by Fr Dumitru Stăniloae in the fourth volume of his systematic theology. He describes the descent of the Spirit as the means by which Christ's saving work extends to human beings, giving life to the Church, which he says is 'the first faithful in whom the power of Christ's pneumatized body is extended'.[3] This leads him to the striking claim that 'without the Church Christ's saving work could not be accomplished.'[4] It is not that Fr Stăniloae has somehow got things backwards here in relation to humanity and salvation; rather it points to a vision of salvation that prioritizes the role of the Spirit in manifesting the work of Christ in us. The presence of the Spirit is inseparable from the presence and work of Christ, for it is the Spirit who fashions us more and more into the likeness of the Son. In this, Fr Stăniloae's thinking might be said to bear significant resemblance to John Wesley's reflections on the Spirit and our sanctification.

Why the difference?

Orthodox polemicists often suggest that the Western tradition's poorer understanding of the life and work of the Holy Spirit is due to the addition of a phrase in the Nicene Creed. In the Western Churches, the Nicene Creed says, 'We believe in the Holy Spirit, the Lord, the giver of life, who proceeds from the Father and the Son.' The phrase 'and the Son' (Latin, *filioque*) in this clause was added to the text of the creed at the Council of Toledo in 539 and was widely accepted into the texts used in the Western Church. It became normative in the English Church following the Council of Hatfield in 680. The Greek-speaking East never accepted this addition to the text of the creed, and over time the disagreement contributed to the Great Schism of 1054. Following a long ecumenical journey, and owing to the close relationship between the Church of England and the Eastern Churches in the twentieth century, there have been moves to drop the *filioque* clause. This was recommended by the Lambeth Conference of 1988, and various member churches of the Anglican Communion no longer use it in the text of the creed. In the Church of England, our canons currently permit both variations.

The theological issue at stake is whether the Holy Spirit proceeds from the Father, or from the Father and the Son. It is an issue of Trinitarian theology. The Anglican position following the Dublin Statement of 1984 is that the so-called 'Double Procession' of the Holy Spirit is not a dogma required of Christians, but that it is an acceptable belief. In essence, the Church, both East and West, equally holds to the Trinitarian faith in its essentials. Nevertheless, there are good historical and ecumenical reasons for removing the *filioque* clause. Given there is no substantial difference to our understanding of the Holy Spirit, we would do well to recover the vitality and dynamism of Orthodoxy's vision of the Spirit at work in the life of the Church and in every Christian.

St Symeon the New Theologian and the Holy Spirit

One of the writers who can give us real insight into the dynamic nature of the Spirit at work is St Symeon the New Theologian. Despite being called 'the New Theologian', St Symeon is not all that new. He was born in the middle of the tenth century, but the saintly title he has been given distinguishes him from the two other saints who are called 'the Theologian', namely the Apostle John and Gregory of Nazianzus. By giving him the title 'the New Theologian', the Church is saying that Symeon is a theological heavyweight, someone whose thinking needs to be grappled with. That might conjure up for us images of dusty tomes and fussy, precise arguments about the language we use about God, but Symeon's theology is a 'mystical theology' rooted in the direct experience of God. His writings are punchy and direct, written in the street Greek of the time. And this got him into trouble. Symeon was a strong personality, who dedicated his life to revivifying the spiritual life of his monastery, and more than once he had to face down a rebellion from his monks. He also attracted the ire of the chief theologian of the court of the Byzantine Emperor, Archbishop Stephen of Nicomedia. Stephen thought that Symeon was too 'Charismatic' and that his emphasis on the direct experience of the Holy Spirit undermined the structures of the Church and the authority of the clergy. This, of course, is a tension that has resurfaced again and again in the history of the Church! One particularly controversial issue was Symeon's claim that it was possible for non-ordained monks to hear confessions and forgive sins. He said that in order to impart the Holy Spirit, it is necessary to possess the Holy Spirit through purity of life, and that the secular bishops and priests had lost the Holy Spirit through their moral corruption. It is easy to see how Symeon might have got on Archbishop Stephen's nerves. This dispute came to a head in 1009 and Symeon was forced into exile before he was finally vindicated and allowed to return.

It is true that Symeon's emphasis on mystical experience means that his language is often not very precise, and if pushed to its logical conclusion might lead to somewhat unorthodox positions. But this is to misunderstand him. His writings are deeply rooted in the Scriptures and in the Church Fathers, and it is important to understand the urgency of his task, encouraging his monks to that renewed conversion and the indwelling of the Holy Spirit. This required a deep, personal and emotional connection. And Symeon knew that his monks would be won over by hearing his experiences and the experiences of others, and not by precise theological formulations. Symeon's basic conviction is that the knowledge of God doesn't come from books, but rather from living the spiritual life and the experience of God in prayer.

In a text written for his monks, Symeon tells the veiled auto-biographical story of a young man, about 20 years old and living in Constantinople, who became a disciple of a holy monk, and was balancing a secular life during the day with an intense prayer life during the night.[5] At the age of 14, Symeon sought out the spiritual elder of the Stoudios monastery in Constantinople, St Symeon the Studite, who became his spiritual guide. The younger Symeon was told that he should wait before committing himself to the monastery, so he lived a double life managing the household of a wealthy patrician and praying and studying spiritual writings. He received a number of spiritual graces during this period of his life. In the autobiographical account, Symeon describes the experience of a flood of Divine Light that seemed so overwhelming that he felt that he had somehow been trans-formed into the Divine Light. And this brief mystical experience changed his life.

Light is important in the Christian mystical tradition. We might think of the light of the Transfiguration, or of the light that sur-rounds St Paul in his vision on the road to Damascus. Symeon returns again and again to this image of the Divine Light in his writings. In one of his *Hymns of Divine Love*, he writes,

For I was seated in the light of a lamp that was shining on me. And it was illuminating the darkness and the shadows of night. It seemed indeed to me that in the light I was occupied in reading, but as if I were scrutinizing the words and examining the propositions. Then as I was meditating, Master, on these things, suddenly You appeared from above, much greater than the sun and You shone brilliantly from the heavens down into my heart. But all the rest, I was seeing as a deep shadow.[6]

Light exposes the reality of things, allowing us to see things as they really are, and all the rest is shadow. But crucially, for Symeon this experience is transformative. It is not static, and the light that shines on us and changes us is an important reminder that God cannot be contained. And importantly, Symeon is clear that this mystical encounter with God is accessible to everybody, regardless of their age or state in life. Reflecting on his own experience, the young Symeon who had a worldly job in a busy city hadn't gone into the desert, or up a pillar or into a cave. And yet, as a young man, he encountered the Divine Light and the transforming grace of the Holy Spirit. The experience of God is not just for monks in their monasteries, but through repentance and conversion of heart, we can all come to the vision of the Divine Light that Symeon describes.

There is something profoundly freeing about Symeon's vision of a God who comes to us, enlightening our hearts and minds and transforming us by his divine presence. It is a wild, almost anarchic vision, recalling Jesus' words in John 3.8: 'The wind blows wherever it pleases. You hear its sound, but you cannot tell where it comes from or where it is going. So it is with everyone who is born of the Spirit.' In Symeon's life and writings, we see the clash between a living, experiential model of theology and a rationalistic, institutional, intellectual one. But Symeon shows us above all the importance of a personal, transformative encounter, a living relationship. Like Symeon, we may come up against the rigidness of the institutional Church, but the Spirit is always at work, moulding, illuminating and changing our lives.

Acquiring the Holy Spirit: St Seraphim of Sarov

In November 1831, a young Russian nobleman, Nikolai Aleksandrovich Motovilov, went into the woods near Sarov, between Moscow and Kazan. He was looking to meet with a spiritual elder, much in the way that the young St Symeon had sought out St Symeon the Studite. The elder whom he met was the now widely venerated St Seraphim of Sarov.

St Seraphim was born in 1754 in central Russia, the son of a builder. As a child, he fell from the roof of a church that his father had been working on but escaped unscathed. He said that a lady caught him in her shawl and lowered him to the ground. He had a second brush with death, this time through illness, but he had a vision of the Mother of God and was cured after venerating a miraculous icon. So, from his childhood, his deep piety and devotion led him to the monastic life. For a period of about 30 years altogether, he lived as a hermit in the forest around Sarov. Seraphim is often depicted in his icon with a bear, with whom he was great friends, much to the shock and horror of the Reverend Mother of the community of nuns in Seraphim's care! At one time, he was beaten by robbers, who left him for dead. Seraphim had another vision of the Virgin Mary, and his body began to heal. After ten more years of solitary life, he opened the door of his cell to visitors and received countless pilgrims who came to him for advice, prayer and healing. Nikolai Aleksandrovich Motovilov was one such visitor.

Motovilov wrote down accounts of his conversations with St Seraphim and became a devoted follower. His manuscripts were largely unpublished in his lifetime, but his widow preserved them in a basket in the attic, covered in dust and pigeon droppings, and eventually gave them to a writer to work on and publish. The preservation of these writings is, in itself, miraculous: St Seraphim's teachings would not have reached so wide a public without them.

St Seraphim's spirituality is characterized by a joy and simplicity, and so he is often compared with St Francis of Assisi (a comparison enhanced by the incident with the bear!). He used to address the people he met as 'My joy!' or 'Lover of God'. His humility is widely documented by Motovilov and by the nuns to whom he was a spiritual father. But that conversation in the woods in late November 1831 is a powerful testament to St Seraphim's belief in the power and presence of the Holy Spirit in the life of every Christian.

He begins his instruction to Motovilov with a striking interpretation of Scripture. He quotes a verse that doesn't actually exist anywhere in the New Testament: 'the Apostle [Paul] writes,

"We set off to Achaia and the Holy Spirit did not go with us, we returned to Macedonia and the Holy Spirit went with us!"' My best guess is that 'Achaia' is a mistake for 'Asia' and that this is in fact a summary of what happens to Paul and Timothy in Acts 16, where their journey is dictated by the Holy Spirit:

> They went through the region of Phrygia and Galatia, having been forbidden by the Holy Spirit to speak the word in Asia. When they had come opposite Mysia, they attempted to go to Bithynia, but the Spirit of Jesus did not allow them. (Acts 16.6–7)

Paul then has a vision, inspired by the Holy Spirit, of a Macedonian man pleading for help that leads them to preach the Good News in Macedonia. St Seraphim explores how Paul can be so confident of the promptings and direction of the Spirit:

> Now some say this passage is incomprehensible, because surely the Apostles could not so obviously sense the Holy Spirit with them. Is there not some mistake here? But, Lover of God, there was no mistake and there is none, for the Holy Apostles really were always able to see the Holy Spirit with them in this way.[7]

He suggests that the Holy Spirit was a visible and tangible presence to the Apostles after Pentecost. St Seraphim then outlines the idea that the Spirit was visibly present in Adam after God breathed into him the Breath of Life, but that this precious gift was lost after the Fall. The Spirit departed. This makes sense of John 7.39, 'for as yet there was no Spirit, because Jesus was not yet glorified'. Seraphim tells us that while the actions of the Holy Spirit were discernible in the world (as seen in the words of Scripture and even in the pagan philosophers), it is only with the Incarnation, death and Resurrection of Jesus that the Spirit again comes into the world. The Risen Jesus breathes into the disciples the same Breath of Life that God breathed into Adam, and the same Spirit is breathed into us at our baptism.

There are a number of things in this conversation that challenge our usual ways of understanding the work of the Holy Spirit, not least the idea that the Spirit can depart from us. But I think that the idea of the visible and tangible presence of the Holy Spirit is worth exploring. We are very used to describing the Spirit as ineffable and uncontainable. We reach for images and metaphors. There's a children's book by Leslie Francis and Nicola Slee, part of a series about a bear called Teddy Horsley, called *The Windy Day*. It shows how Teddy Horsley cannot see or hear or feel the wind, but he can see and hear and feel the effects of the wind. When he goes to church for Pentecost, he realizes that he cannot see or hear or feel the Holy Spirit, but that he sees and hears and feels the action of the Spirit around him. This is probably how we too have thought about the Holy Spirit. But St Seraphim's teaching encourages us to be a lot bolder and more radical in our understanding of the Spirit. It is our lack of perception, our vision clouded by sin, that means we fail to see God's Holy Spirit in us and among us.

St Seraphim famously says, 'the aim of the Christian life consists in acquiring the Spirit of God.'[8] We must open our eyes and attune ourselves to the reality of the Spirit's presence in us through the grace we receive at baptism. He says that we can acquire the Spirit through good deeds done for the sake of Christ, and above all through prayer: 'Lover of God, prayer more than anything brings the Holy Spirit, and prayer is open to anyone.'[9] We see an echo here of St Symeon's teaching that the mystical encounter with God is accessible to everyone, regardless of their age and state of life. The spiritual life is not just reserved for the professionally religious. God's greatest gift, God's very presence, is freely given to us when we learn to pray.

Over the course of Motovilov's conversation with St Seraphim, the elder's eyes seemed to flash like lightning and his face shone more brightly than the sun. The same light engulfed Motovilov too, and he felt an indescribable peace in his soul. We can see the similarity in the teaching of St Symeon the New Theologian who connects the very presence of the Spirit with this transforming and transformative Divine Light. The action of the Holy Spirit in the world is not an abstract idea, but a real transfiguration of all created things, beginning with each individual human person. We see more clearly through this lens what Fr Stăniloae meant when he wrote that the Spirit extends the 'power of Christ's pneumatized body' to the Church, to every Christian. Through their experience of the Divine Light, St Symeon the New Theologian and St Seraphim of Sarov show us the way that the Holy Spirit brings to fruition the work of the Resurrection in us, uniting our lives for ever with Christ's risen life. The Spirit's presence literally illumined the physical bodies of these two great mystics, foreshadowing in their earthly lives their ultimate and eternal union with God. We may never have this kind of dramatic mystical experience ourselves, but we might with John Wesley feel our hearts strangely warmed. The experience of the presence of the Spirit bringing light and warmth and peace to our hearts and minds is something we might well recognize. The Orthodox tradition equips us to see this as not just a 'fuzzy feeling' but the action of God in us, forming us into the life of Christ and preparing us for eternity.

Orthodoxy: Pentecostal and Charismatic

St Symeon the New Theologian and St Seraphim of Sarov, separated by time and place, offer us a profound vision of the Holy Spirit at work. They help us to understand the Pentecostal and Charismatic nature of Orthodox spirituality, as the Spirit forms us ever more into the likeness of Christ. It is an understanding of the Spirit and the Church that takes us back to the moment of Pentecost, inspires our mission and makes manifest the Kingdom. If we have any experience of Orthodoxy and of worship in the Pentecostal churches, we might think that these ecclesial traditions are simply poles apart. But in recent years, there has been some extraordinary ecumenical and theological dialogue between the Pentecostal churches and the Orthodox Church, at both unofficial and official levels. These discussions have centred on questions such as the nature of spiritual experience, mission as healing and reconciliation, authority and charism in the life of the Church, and the discernment of holiness. There has been a move in academic Pentecostal circles to study the writings of the Church Fathers, and an increasing liturgical awareness within Pentecostalism. Similarly, there has been academic engagement on the Orthodox side in Pentecostal theology, for instance comparing St Symeon the New Theologian's view of baptism in the Holy Spirit with the theological thinking of Pentecostal theologians like Simon Chan or Frank Macchia.[10] Neither side is naive about the differences that exist between Orthodox and Pentecostal expressions of the Christian faith, but this is a fruitful dialogue from which other Christian denominations can learn a lot.

Ultimately, the Orthodox tradition challenges the Church to embrace a richer and more profound understanding of the Holy Spirit, drawing all creation to share in the divine life of the Holy Trinity. We should not relegate our thinking and preaching about the Spirit to the time between the Ascension and Pentecost. Rather, we should open our eyes to the real, tangible and transforming presence of the Holy Spirit in our lives. We should open our hearts and minds to the Spirit's illuminating grace, to the work of Christ in us, that we might know the peace, love and joy that is our hope and our destiny.

Heavenly King, Comforter, Spirit of Truth; you are everywhere present and fill all things. Treasury of blessings and Giver of Life, come and dwell within in us; cleanse us of all stain; and save our souls O Gracious One.

Notes

1 Thomas Jackson, ed., 1984, *The Works of John Wesley*, vol. 10, reprint, Ada, MI: Baker Book House, p. 82.

2 Revd John Brownlie in fact translated four volumes of hymns from the Eastern Church.

3 Dumitru Stăniloae, 2012, *The Experience of God: Orthodox Dogmatic Theology*, vol. 4, Brookline, MA: Holy Cross Orthodox Press, p. 2.

4 Stăniloae, *The Experience of God: Orthodox Dogmatic Theology*, vol. 4, p. 2.

5 Recounted as happening to a certain man called George, following the example of Paul in 2 Cor. 12, relating a mystical experience in the third person. Gerald Palmer, Kallistos Ware and Philip Sherrard, trans., 1999, *The Philokalia: The Complete Text*, vol. 4, London: Faber and Faber, pp. 16–24.

6 George Maloney, trans., 1978, *Hymns of Divine Love by St Symeon the New Theologian*, Denville, NJ: Dimension Books, p. 135.

7 John Philips, trans., 2010, *The Aim of the Christian Life: The Conversation of St Seraphim of Sarov with N.A. Motovilov*, Cambridge: Saints Alive Press, p. 9.

8 Philips, trans., *The Aim of the Christian Life*, p. 22.

9 Philips, trans., *The Aim of the Christian Life*, p. 29.

10 Mihai-Iulian Grobnicu, 2016, 'Baptism in the Holy Spirit – An Analysis of the Doctrine at Symeon the New Theologian and in Classical Pentecostal Movement', *International Journal of Orthodox Theology*, 7(4), pp. 166–204.

Conclusion

It may seem surprising that many of the themes we have considered in this book on Orthodox spirituality are broadly familiar to us: images of the saints, the liturgical tradition, hymn-singing and Scripture. Even the *Philokalia*'s call to self-examination and a deeper self-knowledge has parallels in the Western monastic tradition. These form part of our shared inheritance that stretches back to the early days of Christianity. The Orthodox tradition, however, challenges us to see these things in new ways and from different angles. It presents us with different emphases and concerns, a different grammar and vocabulary for understanding the nature of God, the Church and the world.

The spirituality of the Eastern Churches developed in different geographical, political, intellectual and religious contexts to Christianity in the West. There are myriad ways of accounting for the differences between Orthodoxy and the Catholic or Protestant Churches: the political domination of the Ottomans in the Balkans, a lack of centralized authority, the limited influence of the Protestant Reformation or the philosophy of the European Enlightenment. Any one of these factors, however, will only give a partial answer. And, of course, there are differences between Orthodox jurisdictions, and between the homelands of Orthodoxy and the diaspora communities.

For Anglican, Roman Catholic and Protestant Christians, the Orthodox tradition holds before us a lens through which we can see those parts of our common heritage in a new light. This journey of discovery may lead some people into the full communion of the Orthodox Church, but it will be different for those of us on the outside who nevertheless value the Orthodox Church's spiritual gifts. We are unlikely to adopt the Liturgy of St John Chrysostom in our churches or start using Byzantine chant for the psalms at evensong. We can, however, enrich our spiritual lives through this journey of discovery. And in this, there is no substitute for a real and genuine encounter with the Orthodox faith in its lived expression among Orthodox Christians. It may feel like a step into the unknown, but visiting an Orthodox parish for the Liturgy (particularly over a period of time) is better than reading any number of books on Orthodox spirituality. A personal encounter is at the heart of all our strivings for unity. In 1970, Fr Dumitru Stăniloae gave a series of addresses for the Anglican Sisters of the Love of God at Fairacres in Oxford.[1] In his introduction to the published volume of these addresses, Donald Allchin remarked on the depth of unity that emerged in the discussions that followed the talks: the Sisters, formed by the Carmelite spirituality of sixteenth-century Spain, and a Franciscan visitor, rooted in the mendicant spirituality of St Francis, both remarked on the way that Fr Stăniloae's Orthodoxy illumined new aspects of their own spiritual traditions.[2] Allchin wrote,

We can see not only something of the unifying power of the Orthodox tradition at its deepest and best, but also something of the way in which the ecumenical dialogue between the Churches must be carried on. The questions of dogmatic theology cannot and must not be avoided. But they need to be met at the place where theology and spirituality come together into one. When they are seen in relation to the living and praying experience of the Christian people, then we find unexpected possibilities of reconciliation between positions which appear at first sight to be absolutely opposed. Where the mind is being re-established in the heart ... there understanding and deep agreement becomes possible.[3]

For his part, Fr Stăniloae said on this occasion,

[I have found here] a love and care which goes beyond anything I could imagine. I have found a family here ... in which I have found a complete convergence of thought and desire with that of my own heart and mind.[4]

There really is no substitute for the personal encounter and it is my hope that readers of this book will take the time to make a personal connection with their local Orthodox churches.

Nevertheless, I also hope this book has shown some of the potential for integrating these insights into our own spiritual lives, regardless of the church traditions from which we come. Far from being exotic or mystical or foreign, even, the spiritual treasures of the Orthodox Church are part of our inheritance too because of our fundamental unity in Christ. Sometimes the light they shed on our own traditions, customs and practices will challenge us. They will make us think twice about our approach to images, or the nature of congregational participation in worship, for instance. This is no bad thing. It always does us good to see things from new perspectives, even where we disagree. Our own understanding and vision are enhanced by the things that are different as well as the things that are similar. But through a sustained engagement with the Orthodox tradition, we learn to discover that we share much more than we might have first thought. And we can learn to see those things afresh, perhaps even more clearly.

Over the course of this book, we have considered Orthodox spirituality through five themes: icons; the *Philokalia*; the Divine Liturgy; Byzantine hymnody; and the image of the Divine Light. Each of these aspects of Orthodox spirituality can be of benefit to us in our prayer lives.

In our chapter on icons, we explored the way that icons can help us concentrate in prayer, fixing our gaze on God. This process can help us be more attentive to what we see around us in our daily lives, helping us to overcome distractions not only in our prayer, but also in our relationships and our engagement with the world around us. More than this, learning to fix our gaze on God also allows us to be seen, to understand that we are known and loved beyond measure.

The *Philokalia* is perhaps the most unfamiliar of the themes we have considered in this book, but there is much wisdom for us in its many pages. As well as some very sound practical advice on how to pray, taking into account our posture and our breathing, the *Philokalia* also gives us the language of the 'passions' through which we can better understand ourselves. This search for self-knowledge requires humility, but through it we can grow more and more into the likeness of Christ.

The Orthodox approach to the Liturgy reminds us that human beings are made for worship: we are made to respond in love to the God who created us and who draws us to share in the divine life. When Christians gather in worship, we see a glimpse of heaven and the vision of a redeemed community transfigured by Christ's Resurrection. The Orthodox tradition challenges us to hold this vision before us in order that our worship can make visible the Resurrection within the walls of the church, and also beyond them in the societies and communities in which we live.

Byzantine chant sounds exotic to Western ears because of the different musical traditions that developed over the centuries. While Byzantine hymnody sounds very different from the hymnody of the Western Churches, and often has a different liturgical function, we have seen the ways that Byzantine hymns can challenge us to rethink biblical stories. They invite us to contemplate the Scriptures more deeply and to make the text of Scripture part of our own stories. The tradition of Byzantine hymn writing reminds us that hymns can be a rich source for prayer and theological reflection. We can use hymns devotionally to enrich our communal worship and our private prayer.

Last, we considered the theme of Divine Light in the mystical experiences of two great saints separated by time and geography, St Symeon the New Theologian and St Seraphim of Sarov. These mystical experiences show the important role of the Holy Spirit in Orthodox belief and practice, which can sometimes be neglected in Western Christian traditions. The encounters with

Divine Light highlight the Spirit's tangible presence in the world, bringing to fruition the redeeming work of Christ in each of us. Thus the Orthodox tradition invites us to keep our eyes open to the promptings of the Spirit, to see the Spirit at work and to be transformed by the Spirit.

For those outside the Orthodox Church, the Orthodox tradition can seem dauntingly unfamiliar at best or mired in obscurantism and geopolitics at worst. However, if we get to know Orthodox communities and practices, we can discover spiritual treasures that help us to see things in new ways, making visible the transforming power of Christ's Resurrection, and drawing us into the life of the Kingdom of God in the here and now.

Notes

1 Dumitru Stăniloae, 2023, *The Victory of the Cross*, third edition, Oxford: SLG Press.
2 Stăniloae, *The Victory of the Cross*, pp. 2–3.
3 Allchin, in Stăniloae, *The Victory of the Cross*, p. 3.
4 Stăniloae, *The Victory of the Cross*, p. 4.

Bibliography

Barrington-Ward, Simon, 2007, *The Jesus Prayer*, Abingdon: BRF.

Bel, Valer and Preda, Radu, 2013, 'The Development of Missionary and Social Studies' in Viorel Ioniţă, ed., *Orthodox Theology in the 20th Century and Early 21st Century: A Romanian Orthodox Perspective*, Bucharest: Basilica, pp. 701–70.

Bria, Ion, 1978, 'The Liturgy after the Liturgy', *International Review of Mission*, 67, pp. 86–90.

Brock, Sebastian, trans., 2012, *Treasure-house of Mysteries: Explorations of the Sacred Text through Poetry in the Syriac Tradition*, New York: SVS Press.

Bulgakov, Sergius, 2009, *The Burning Bush: On the Orthodox Veneration of the Mother of God*, Grand Rapids, MI: William B. Eerdmans Publishing Company.

Chambers, Peter, trans., 1989, *Nicodemos of the Holy Mountain: A Handbook of Spiritual Counsel*, Classics of Western Spirituality, Mahwah, NJ: Paulist Press.

Edmonds, Rosemary, trans., 2020, *St Sophrony, On Prayer: Reflections of a Modern Saint*, New York: SVS Press.

Foucault, Michel, 1986, *The Care of the Self: Volume 3 of the History of Sexuality*, New York: Pantheon Books.

French, Reginald Michael, trans., 1995, *The Way of a Pilgrim: A Classic of Orthodox Spirituality*, London: SPCK.

Frost, David, trans., 2015, *Divine Liturgy of St John Chrysostom*, Cambridge: IOCS.

Grillaert, Nel, 2011, '"Raise the People in Silence": Traces of Hesychasm in Dostoevskij's Fictional Saint Zosima', *Dostoevsky Studies*, New Series, 15, pp. 47–88.

Grobnicu, Mihai-Iulian, 2016, 'Baptism in the Holy Spirit – An Analysis of the Doctrine at Symeon the New Theologian and in Classical Pentecostal Movement', *International Journal of Orthodox Theology*, 7(4), pp. 166–204.

Harvey, Susan Ashbrook, 2006, *Scenting Salvation: Ancient Christianity and the Olfactory Imagination*, Oakland, CA: University of California Press.

Hatfield, Chad, 2022, 'The Eucharist as Antidote to Secularism: Insights from a Twentieth-Century American Orthodox Perspective' in Daniel Munteanu and Sorin Şelaru, eds, *Holding Fast to the Mystery of Faith: Festschrift for Patriarch Daniel of the Romanian Orthodox Church*, Leiden: Brill, pp. 223–9.

Jackson, Thomas, ed., 1984, *The Works of John Wesley*, vol. 10, reprint, Ada, MI: Baker Book House.

Lebreton, Christophe, 2014, *Born from the Gaze of God: The Tibhirine Journal of a Martyr Monk (1993–1996)*, Collegeville, PA: Cistercian Publications.

Lingas, Alexander, and Cappella Romana, 2021, *Hymns of Kassiani*, Bristol: Cappella Records.

Louth, Andrew, trans., 2003, *John of Damascus: Three Treatises on the Divine Images*, New York: SVS Press.

Louth, Andrew, 2015, *Modern Orthodox Thinkers: From the Philokalia to the Present*, London: SPCK.

Maloney, George, trans., 1978, *Hymns of Divine Love by St Symeon the New Theologian*, Denville, NJ: Dimension Books.

Mellas, Andrew, 2020, *Liturgy and the Emotions in Byzantium: Compunction and Hymnody*, Cambridge: Cambridge University Press.

Mellas, Andrew, trans., 2020, *Hymns of Repentance: Saint Romanos the Melodist*, New York: SVS Press.

Mother Mary and Ware, Kallistos, trans., 2002, *The Lenten Triodion*, reprint, Waymart, PA: St Tikhon's Seminary Press.

Nouwen, Henri, 1987, *Behold the Beauty of the Lord: Praying with Icons*, Notre Dame, IN: Ave Maria Press.

Nouwen, Henri, 1992, *The Return of the Prodigal Son: A Story of Homecoming*, London: Darton, Longman and Todd.

Ouspensky, Leonid, 1992, *Theology of the Icon*, vol. 1, New York: SVS Press.

Palmer, Gerald, Ware, Kallistos and Sherrard, Philip, trans., 1979–2024, *The Philokalia: The Complete Text*, vols. 1–5, London: Faber and Faber.

Papavassiliou, Vassilios, 2012, *Journey to the Kingdom: An Insider's Look at the Liturgy and Beliefs of the Eastern Orthodox Church*, Brewster: Paraclete Press.

Pevear, Richard and Volokhonsky, Larissa, trans., 2003, *Mother Maria Skobtsova: Essential Writings*, Modern Spiritual Masters Series, Maryknoll, NY: Orbis Books.

Philips, John, trans., 2010, *The Aim of the Christian Life: The Conversation of St Seraphim of Sarov with N.A. Motovilov*, Cambridge: Saints Alive Press.

Schmemann, Alexander, 1998, *For the Life of the World: Sacraments and Orthodoxy*, New York: SVS Press.

Sonea, Cristian, 2020, 'The "Liturgy after the Liturgy" and Deep Solidarity: The Orthodox Understanding of Christian Witness and its Implications for Human Society', *Mission Studies*, 37, pp. 452–77.

Stăniloae, Dumitru, 2012, *The Experience of God: Orthodox Dogmatic Theology*, vol. 4, Brookline: Holy Cross Orthodox Press.

Stăniloae, Dumitru, 2023, *The Victory of the Cross*, third edition, Oxford: SLG Press.

Twisleton, John, 2014, *Using the Jesus Prayer: Steps to a Simpler Christian life*, Abingdon: BRF.

Williams, Rowan, 2021, *Looking East in Winter: Contemporary Thought and the Eastern Christian Tradition*, London: Bloomsbury Continuum.

Williams, Rowan, 2024, *Passions of the Soul*, London: Bloomsbury Continuum.

www.ingramcontent.com/pod-product-compliance
Lightning Source LLC
LaVergne TN
LVHW092144120626

841161LV00030B/387